MAY 0 4 2011

ANIMAL RIGHTS

WHAT EVERYONE NEEDS TO KNOW

D0979812

ANIMAL RIGHTS
WHAT EVERYONE NEEDS TO KNOW

PAUL WALDAU

OXFORD
UNIVERSITY PRESS

2011

OXFORD
UNIVERSITY PRESS

Oxford University Press, Inc., publishes works that further
Oxford University's objective of excellence
in research, scholarship, and education.

Oxford   New York
Auckland   Cape Town   Dar es Salaam   Hong Kong   Karachi
Kuala Lumpur   Madrid   Melbourne   Mexico City   Nairobi
New Delhi   Shanghai   Taipei   Toronto

With offices in
Argentina   Austria   Brazil   Chile   Czech Republic   France   Greece
Guatemala   Hungary   Italy   Japan   Poland   Portugal   Singapore
South Korea   Switzerland   Thailand   Turkey   Ukraine   Vietnam

Copyright © 2011 by Oxford University Press, Inc.

Published by Oxford University Press, Inc.
198 Madison Avenue, New York, NY 10016

www.oup.com

Oxford is a registered trademark of Oxford University Press

All rights reserved. No part of this publication may be reproduced,
stored in a retrieval system, or transmitted, in any form or by any means,
electronic, mechanical, photocopying, recording, or otherwise,
without the prior permission of Oxford University Press.

Library of Congress Cataloging-in-Publication Data
Waldau, Paul.
Animal rights : what everyone needs to know / Paul Waldau.
p.   cm.
Includes index.
ISBN 978-0-19-973997-4; 978-0-19-973996-7 (pbk.)
1. Animal rights.
I. Title.
HV4708.W35 2010
179'.3—dc22   2010011035

1 3 5 7 9 8 6 4 2

Printed in the United States of America
on acid-free paper

CONTENTS

PREFACE

As I contemplated how to answer the question "What do people need to know?" about the important but controversial notion of animal rights, I considered three things. First, I thought of the hundreds, perhaps thousands, of conversations on this topic that I have had with people in ordinary walks of life from all over the world. These have helped me appreciate the great variety of views on this topic.

Second, I thought about what I had learned during several decades of studying animal topics in various educational contexts. I spent years in Oxford, England, studying the academic side of various issues, and I then spent a decade teaching in a veterinary school. At about the same time, I taught the subject of "animal law" at some of my country's best law schools. I also had the privilege of lecturing at dozens of universities and law schools as well as in public conferences, before thousands of people.

Third, I looked at hundreds of books, printed articles and Web sites that used the phrase "animal rights" because I wanted to see whether people were talking to—or past—one another.

Based on all of this background and research, I came to the conclusion that the following issues are the most important ones, and thus "what everyone needs to know," about animal rights.

Animal rights is an ancient topic that recently has taken a special twist. The phrase "animal rights" has been, and still is, employed most often to describe *moral rights* and social values in favor of compassion and against cruelty. The modern twist is the emergence of conversations where the term means all of this *and more*, namely, the possibility of *legal rights* for some or all nonhuman animals. The latter are important protections, and today there is a very active debate over how often and to what extent our different human societies might put specific legal rights and other protections into place for specific animals.

This debate about "animal rights" as "specific legal rights" colors what many influential people say about the term, but this special and, I think, important sense of the term still remains secondary to the more generic meaning of "moral protections." This book tries to explain why "animal rights" in the sense of moral rights is the larger and more fundamental issue, and why specific legal rights for specific nonhuman individuals reflects, but does not encompass all of, animal rights as moral rights.

Second, the debate over animal rights often is polarized, but only in some circles. In those places where polarization impacts how people talk and hear one another as this issue is discussed, the advocates and activists at opposite ends of the long continuum of views continue to debate in ways that fuel even further polarization.

Third and most relevant to today's use of "animal rights," I found that many people do connect with each other when talking about animal rights. Further, many people recognize discussions about "animal rights" as *pro-people.* This conclusion will seem counterintuitive to some, perhaps even an outright falsehood to others. But if you explore the debates over animal rights at length, you will notice that those who make the claim that animal rights can be pro-people argue their point in several different ways. Some argue this must be so because humans are "animals." Others argue that talk of animal rights affirms life, which of course has decidedly pro-human features. Still others argue that concerns to protect the living beings outside our own species honor *humans* in a special way by, first, affirming and, second, strengthening *our* ethical nature.

Lots of people also sense that the phrase "animal rights" is not a complicated phrase, but instead a phrase that easily and naturally means something very simple and basic along the lines of "protections for other living beings." Others think the phrase most truly means "we should listen to the voice of animals." Veterinary students often told me that "animal rights" is "a valuable term," but when they use it they risk condemnation by some classmates and, tragically, members of their veterinary school faculty and administration.

Many people feel "animal rights" has undeniable appeal but that it is compromised whenever animal activists use violence on behalf of "the cause." Quite a few who mentioned violence commented on how rare such violence was, and then answered their own concerns by asking out loud, "Why let a few violent people control whether we use a term that describes a movement that was originally nonviolent and today remains overwhelmingly so?"

Today, as this book shows, animal protection is a worldwide social movement. At times, active citizens in this movement challenge deeply cherished values and long-standing practices. Some other citizens react strongly to such challenges, which suggests that the risk of polarization is not going to disappear, no matter how effective this book or any other single volume is at getting all of us to talk fairly, fully, and respectfully about the basic issue of our relationships with the life out beyond the species line.

What is most sorely needed is a willingness to recognize that the debate over "animal rights" is one in which fundamental values are being worked out. Without question, some people feel strongly that mere mention of the topic is a repudiation of humans and thus deeply immoral. But I found that many more people feel this kind of thinking focused solely on humans falls short of humans' ethical possibilities.

Thus I think people need to know how many people find multiple connections with the world in concerns for "animal rights." Because the phrase works for so many *not as a repudiation of humans* but as an affirmation of humans' special abilities to care about others, whether those "others" be human or other-than-human, the phrase opens doors to the rich, more-than-human world that is out beyond our species. For them, animal rights is a win-win situation, not an either/or matter.

Particularly revealing about those people who find the notion of animal rights to be a connecting one, rather than a disconnecting one, is the range of connections affirmed by "animal rights." Of course, one set of connections is with other animals. As the English historian Marc Gold wrote in 1995, "The term animal rights is nothing more than a useful kind of shorthand for a movement based on the recognition that nonhuman animals live purposeful emotional lives and are as capable of suffering as humans....kindness and tolerance for those different and weaker than ourselves are amongst the highest possible human aspirations."

But the connections by no means stop there. The phrase "animal rights" also connected people with "nature," "the environment," the local ecological world in and beyond their backyards, and, incredibly, *with other humans in a variety of ways.* Of great significance for the future, it seemed to me, was a pattern of children pushing their parents to consider "the animals."

These connections were not always called out explicitly. Yet even when these connections were only implicit, they were every bit as real, personal, and motivating. Both adults and children found animal rights to be one way to honor the world as, to use a phrase from the recently deceased visionary Thomas Berry, "a communion of subjects, not a collection of objects."

So one point of this book is that *everyone needs to know* that polarization over animal rights need not be the dominant feature of the debate. Instead, the dominant feature of most discussions about animal rights is the common question, "What is the meaning of life?" My experience in exploring the animal rights debate has taught me that people ask this question because they feel emotionally committed to those around them. People recognize that daily actions, choices, and work can express human imagination and our considerable abilities to care, and they know that we thrive when we connect to some larger project which began before our own life and which will continue after it.

Ethical concerns for other living beings, whether human or not, provide such possibilities. Many people today understand "animal rights," however one defines it, to be a path of caring that leads to the fullest possible future. They have found that this form of life not only fosters virtues but in actual practice sustains the prospering of human imagination. My own experience is that in the class, as in life, inquiring beyond the species line prompts healthy, communicative forms of thinking and rationality, rather than the destructive, manipulative, instrumental forms of thinking so characteristic of selfishness and a small soul.

When humans experience others—again, it matters not whether these "others" are human or members of some other species—paradoxically this experience of getting beyond the self allows humans to become as *fully human* as we can be, that is, human in the context of a biologically rich world full of other interesting living beings. As Viktor Frankl said in his influential *Man's Search for Meaning*, "self-actualization is possible only as a side-effect of self-transcendence." This is true not only for human individuals but also for the human species as a whole. This has in fact been the message of many religions, many ethical systems, and various wisdom traditions anchored in small-scale societies.

Through writing this book I came to understand that animal rights, as most people described it to me, is about connecting to the meaning of life.

ANIMAL RIGHTS

WHAT EVERYONE NEEDS TO KNOW

1

GENERAL INFORMATION

In the phrase "animal rights," the word "animal" is rarely, if ever, understood to refer to humans. Instead, it is virtually always a reference to living beings outside our own species. Humans are, of course, primates, mammals, vertebrates, and so forth. Since all of these categories are *animal* categories, it can be said that scientifically humans are "animals" in every sense of the word. Further, since humans clearly have rights (however we end up defining this term), in one minor sense it is true that *everyone* already acknowledges that at least *some* animals (namely, humans) have and deserve rights.

But the driving issue in the animal rights movement discussed in this book is the question of *which other animals*, that is, which other primates, other mammals, other vertebrates, and so on, might also be said to have rights? If the answer to this question is that no others now have them, is it the case that any of the living beings beyond the species line *need* or *deserve* rights of one kind or another?

We later turn in this chapter to more discussion of just who and what fits into the category "animal." Here we turn to some preliminary issues that can be seen better if we look at the other important word in this controversial phrase.

The word "rights" gives virtually any discussion a special quality. Because many people today assume that only humans should have legal rights, controversy can arise when someone claims that various nonhuman animals already have the important protections we call "rights." Some highly respected lawyers today have said, "Without question, they have rights already." Others insist, "They absolutely do *not* have rights today." What is at issue in such discussions about "animal rights," as we will see, is a range of different protections that humans can offer to other living beings.

Why do we need to know what is meant by "animal rights"?

As noted throughout this book, many people in a variety of contexts today easily resort to the word "rights" to signal that something very important is at issue. A major reason for this is the fact that "rights" is an idea that we use when we talk about our own importance as living beings. But for well over a century now, people wishing to protect valued beings *outside* our species have also resorted to talk of "rights" in order to signal the importance of the issue.

So one reason any informed citizen or student of life needs to know what is meant by "animal rights" is that many people use this phrase to signal something very important to them. Examples could be drawn from dozens of societies around the world. Consider one that comes from the internationally known reformer of Islam, Tariq Ramadan. Islam is a religious tradition that began with the Prophet Mohammed, who himself did not talk in terms of "rights." So it is significant when a twenty-first-century reformer of Islam turns to "rights" talk to describe Mohammed's teaching as it impacts contemporary debates over how to kill animals for Islamic ritual use. Ramadan explains in this passage from his 2009 book *Radical Reform* why he is impatient with those people who talk only of technicalities involved when nonhuman animals used in rituals are slaughtered (more on this in chapter 6).

... an animal slaughtered correctly according to Islamic ritual but ill-treated during its lifetime therefore remained, in the light of the Islamic principles transmitted by the Messenger, an anomaly and a betrayal of the message.... The Prophet thus taught that *the animal's right* to be respected, to be spared suffering and given the food it needed, to be well treated, was not negotiable. It was part of human beings' duties and was to be understood as one of the conditions of spiritual elevation.

While the italics here are added, the choice of the word "rights" is representative of both ancient instincts regarding animal protection *and* the manner in which many around the world today talk when they want to emphasize that a particular being or group of beings is important enough to merit concern from us.

But even if it is common to resort to talk about "rights" to explain why something is deeply important, asserting that living beings outside the human species *should* have "rights" produces significant controversy in many circles. This is why it is important to examine (1) how we are now using the term "animal rights," (2) which living beings now have which rights, and (3) the widespread claim that many more animals *should* have rights.

Beyond the fact that some people are now deeply committed to using talk of rights for other living beings, there are other reasons to investigate how "animal rights" is being used. Much communication about this subject is made unduly complicated by the fact that this widely used phrase has a variety of distinctive, even competing meanings. Sometimes the phrase means "moral rights for animals," while at other times the phrase means something far more technical and precise, such as specific *law-based protections* we generally call "legal rights." Both of these senses of "animal rights" are explored in chapter 3 and then, because everyone needs to know the important difference between these two key ideas, throughout the remainder of this book.

Beyond the distinction between moral rights versus legal rights are still other meanings everyone needs to know. In many contexts, "animal rights" is meant to be a generic term for the worldwide social movement that is also known as "the animal protection movement." This is why people who seek to change some contemporary practices involving nonhuman animals are often called "animal rights advocates," even though these advocates often do not seek *legal* rights or even legal changes. Such people may simply be pleading, "Please consider the harms we are doing to this particular group of animals, and if you do consider these harms, you will stop this practice and seek alternatives."

At other times, conscientious citizens who seek only to have *existing* legal protections for nonhuman animals enforced are called "animal rights activists." An example of this form of "animal rights" involves laws against cruelty. While such laws are extremely common, at times local prosecutors for one reason or another choose not to enforce them (this is discussed in chapter 5). Those who push for enforcement of these existing laws have often been charged with pushing for "animal rights."

So anyone in discussions where the term "animal rights" plays a part needs to ask, just what is involved when this term is used? Is the issue a matter of *"moral* rights" or *"legal* rights," or perhaps both? What other adjectives might be placed in front of the word "rights" to clarify just what is at issue? Is someone merely calling for enforcement of existing laws? Are those raising "animal rights" possibly calling attention to a particular harm done to animals that the public would, if informed, find questionable in some way? Or are those labeled "animal rights" protestors really seeking specific, entirely new protections for some group of animals?

Answers to these and other questions suggest two additional reasons everyone needs to know about animal rights. Failure to clarify which sense of "animal rights" a speaker is invoking has often led to people talking past one another. We can avoid many miscommunications and even cases of bad reasoning *if* we take time to clarify the different meanings people give "animal rights" and what is at stake in these different uses.

In addition, *personal* and *society-wide* benefits exist when humans have healthy connections to animals other than members of their own species. Recognizing the animal protection features of one's own cultural heritage is valuable for many reasons, as is recognition of the educational benefits that other animals can have for children and adults. These can be therapeutic personally, but also socially and environmentally because caring about the beings around us, whether human or nonhuman, can lead to increased awareness of the importance of responsible citizenship and responsible consumption. These personal and society-wide benefits are mentioned early here because it is imperative for everyone to know that debates about protecting other living beings are *also debates about humans* living a meaningful, integrated life—we return again and again in this book to the important human side of animal rights issues.

Who, what are "animals"?

There are some prominent, everyday clues to the fact that talking about "animals" can cause problems. If we map the most basic meanings of the word "animal" in our ordinary speech, we find immediately that the word carries two fundamentally different meanings.

The *Oxford English Dictionary*, long the most influential dictionary of the English language, lists "all living beings" as the first definition of "animal." Under this definition, humans clearly fall into the animal category. But the second definition listed reveals another approach entirely to use of the word: "In common usage: one of the lower animals; a brute, or beast, as distinguished from man."

One oddity in the order chosen by the *Oxford English Dictionary* is that the usual practice in defining multiple meanings is to list the most common usage first, followed by less common usage. But in this case, that usual order is reversed. Virtually all dictionaries today cite both of these definitions, although some list first the scientifically accurate use that includes humans, while others list first the use of the term to mean "all living beings *other than humans.*"

The fact that there are two different uses of this key word in our languages is a first clue that talking about "animals" is a contested matter and thus one that can be, in certain circumstances, fraught with challenge and risk. Another relevant clue is related to our commitment to science—in modern societies where science is deeply respected, it is often the case that we give great deference to scientific accuracy. So it is revealing when a common word such as "animal" is used in not only a nonscientific manner but in a manner that actually amounts to an *anti*-scientific statement. Humans are by consensus members of the animal kingdom, and few would contend that humans are not primates or mammals. So one might easily be led to expect that a science-based approach would prevail when we talk about ourselves in the modern world.

But the more common use of the term "animal" is clearly the nonscientific one, which *intentionally excludes* humans, as in the common phrase "humans and animals." This second meaning could be used derogatorily, as in a phrase like "he's no better than an animal." The word "animal" also is common in legal systems, where one almost always finds the term defined to mean "living being outside the human species."

Because there is tension between these two different uses of "animal" in modern societies, the choice one makes between the two can be a sensitive matter. Some people insist on the scientifically correct use, intentionally referring to other living beings as "other animals." When this happens, many who prefer traditional phrases like "humans and animals" understand this speech choice not to be an invocation of scientific values but, instead, a signal of an animal protection agenda.

In reality, favoring *either* choice reveals an agenda. If one chooses the scientifically correct form, that signals that one chooses to come away from the majority practice in order to link humans to other living beings. If one chooses the more common division of living beings into "humans and animals," then one is ignoring the powerful tradition of science and, instead, clearly separating humans from the earth's other living beings. There is no neutral choice at the present time, a fact which offers as yet another clue that talking about "animals" and "animal rights" can be more complex than one might think. In this book, we discuss many other such clues, including the ferment over this issue in education today (chapter 8), the fact that violence is often mentioned in discussions of animal rights (chapter 6), and changing laws around the world (chapter 5).

Where do we find "them"?

When asked about animals, many people first think of those living beings we have come to think of as "pets" or "companion animals" because these animals are thought of as family members in many modern households today. In fact, in many industrialized countries, such as the United States, more households have companion animals than children.

Another category that comes to many people's minds when asked about animals are "wild" animals "out there" beyond our own communities. If you look around, you will notice that wild animals are ubiquitous—they can be found in our cities as domesticated animals gone wild (such as feral cats) or wildlife living nearby or in our backyards. They are sometimes hard to notice, either because they avoid us or are so small as to escape notice. This is one of the reasons that many lives outside our own species are not easy to observe or understand—this is discussed in chapter 2. Such features of wild animals make discussions about "animal rights" a particularly complex subject.

These first two categories—companion animals and wildlife—are in important respects quite different from each other. The first holds but a small number of familiar living beings that share our world, while the second is so diverse and numerous that, as chapter 2 points out, estimating the number of animals "in the wild" is almost impossible. Animals come in many more categories, to be dealt with in chapter 2, such as food animals, research animals, entertainment animals, and work animals.

Is concern for animal rights new?

Animal protection is both ancient and new—it has existed in every culture and religion. Further, concerns for nonhuman animals have taken extremely diverse forms in our many human cultures. This diversity makes the subject of animal protection a very effective tool for teaching about cultural differences. It also makes the subject of animal protection an interesting topic when religious, legal, and ecological differences are discussed. Simply said, concerns for animals have existed from time immemorial, and any human who studies human groups from different times and places will notice almost immediately the extraordinary variety of these concerns.

At the same time, our twenty-first-century experience of the living beings outside our own species has some unique features. A book written in 2002 titled *Dominion: The Power of Man, the Suffering of Animals, and the Call to Mercy* has received much attention because it was written by Matthew Scully, formerly the senior speechwriter of President George W. Bush. The book describes our modern encounter with our fellow living beings as fraught with contradictions: "No age has ever been more solicitous to animals, more curious and caring. Yet no age has ever inflicted upon animals such massive punishments with such complete disregard, as witness scenes to be found on any given day at any modern industrial farm."

Some of the changed circumstances we encounter in this book have come about because we deeply appreciate the many companion animals in our midst. But at the same time we are decimating wildlife locally and internationally. These trends seem incompatible to many, and concern for animals in the companion animal and wildlife category have raised awareness about nonhuman animals in general, all of which has contributed to discomfort about radically new, industrialized forms of raising and slaughtering food animals.

The result is that today's complex milieu of human-animal relationships and concerns for animal protection that seem to some a revolutionary topic, even as such concerns are understood by others to be a traditional topic, handled for thousands of years by religious and ethical traditions. The relationship of these themes is explored in subsequent chapters as history, law, religion, and social values are addressed more fully.

2

THE ANIMALS THEMSELVES

A central issue in any discussion of protections for living beings outside our own species is the question of the animals' actual biological realities. Intuitively, we know that other animals have their own experiences of the world, but some philosophers have aggressively denied that we can know much about these realities (see chapter 3 for more discussion of this issue). Most people, as well as the majority of philosophers, have recognized that we can in fact know *something* of other animals' realities. We have some idea that mammals and some other animals experience pain, and many people are confident they can discern when another animal is suffering. Based on our confidence about such matters, our cultures have for millennia been protecting other animals in a variety of ways, informed by our perception of who and what they are.

While some animals' realities are quite familiar to many people, as in the case of dogs, almost everyone recognizes that some features of nonhumans' lives are very elusive or even unknowable. We consider in the following section what we can reasonably claim to know about other animals, for an answer to this question impacts whether we decide to try to protect them. As part of this inquiry, we need to address some interesting problems that humans inevitably encounter when they set out to know other animals' realities. This inquiry takes us into science and beyond, and will lead us to consider different categories of animals.

What do we know about animals' realities?

In some ways, we know a great deal about other animals. Some of this knowledge is quite simple and basic. Examples include information about the shape of their bodies, the size of their brains, which senses they have, and various features of their reproduction.

Some of our human societies, such as indigenous peoples who hunt other animals, often "know" the habits of other animals in ways that are intricate and detailed compared with the ways citizens in urban cultures "know" other animals. Indigenous peoples may see the claims of citizens in industrialized countries as uninformed when it comes to the daily lives of animals. Nonetheless, people who have been educated in modern school systems clearly have general information about many other animals' lives. They know, for instance, that other living beings are subject to ecological, social, and genetic inputs, just as are our human lives.

We thus know generalities, including where many animals live, what their seasonal patterns are, and which of their senses are dominant. We know that some animals are dominated by their nose or ears, while other animals, like ourselves and our cousin primates, are dominated by vision. So while we might regularly use a phrase like "from that dog's point of *view*," we can appreciate the insight of the scientist Alexandra Horowitz, author of the 2009 book *Inside of a Dog*, when she cleverly employs "From the Dog's Point of *Nose*."

We are inclined to wonder what such animals do with their especially high levels of basic sensory abilities that we also have, but to a far lesser degree. We often know from living with dogs and cats that other animals hear sounds and sniff odors we do not experience. Further, though, we have long realized that some animals have sensory abilities that are altogether different from our own, for we know that some animals, like bats and whales and dolphins, live fully and well with sensory abilities, like echolocation, that are totally foreign to us. In chapter 3, we discuss the important notion of *Umwelt*, which is a concept that careful thinkers about other living beings' realities developed as part of an effort to sort out what it is that we can and cannot know of other animals' worlds.

Our forebears accumulated centuries and even millennia of observations to create impressive classifications of living beings. There are, in fact, many different systems of classification. The science-based tradition, which is called "systematics" (discussed later in this chapter), provides an astonishingly detailed picture of the history and interconnections of life on Earth.

But even if we can say some rather impressive things by virtue of all our classification efforts, it remains clear that we still have much to discover about the lives and communities beyond our own species. For example, while many people feel confident that they know their own dog or cat well enough to tell others about that animal's mind and feelings, it is at best very difficult to know the mental and emotional realities of most other animals.

Some of the problems are obvious—we do not communicate directly with other animals in any precise way, and we are also not around most animals very often. We thus have little relevant information about animals' day-to-day realities as they are experiencing them. Dolphins and whales, for example, spend all of their time in the ocean, and even when we are in a nearby boat and can see them breathe at the surface, we are operating in an environment that is quite alien to us. We may know that they have large brains, live in social groups, and communicate with one another by way of astonishingly complex sound-making abilities, but we know next to nothing about what they do with these abilities.

Whales and dolphins are good examples of animals that teach us that *our* claims about *their* realities should be tempered by realism, lengthy experience, and humility. Simply said, we do not know enough about whales' and dolphins' lives to speak confidently about many, let alone all, the realities of their lives.

Similar problems face us when we try to know the lives and realities of many common animals, such as dogs and cats. We grasp that they have personalities and are distinct from one another, but their inner lives are inaccessible to us in fundamental ways. When asked if they think, we may answer confidently yes, but just what they are doing with that capacity is still heavily disputed.

Limitations on our ability to make claims about other animals are even more applicable to familiar animals that we see often but rarely interact with personally. Birds and small wild mammals like squirrels and foxes, and even the larger mammals like deer that are so common in some areas, are both familiar and alien to us. We recognize them easily, but few of us really know much about their day-to-day lives when they are away from human-dominated places. About animals that are even less familiar to us because we do not see them (perhaps because they are shy or perhaps simply too small for us to notice) or because they live in places alien to us (as fish do), we know even less. Beyond these many limits on what we can claim to "know" about "animals," there are important limits even when we are in the presence of animals that we are studying carefully. These intriguing knowledge problems, put by philosophers into a field known as epistemology (the study of knowledge), are dealt with briefly in chapter 3.

The existence of a significant number of limits on our human knowledge about other living beings is one reason that some people still insist that we must employ a certain amount of humility when we make claims about other living beings, including even those that are most familiar to us. But others assume that human intelligence is the measure of all intelligence, and thus we are in a position to know a great deal about other animals.

However one works out the breathtaking claim that human intelligence is the pinnacle or measure of all intelligence, we can justifiably take pride in our sciences' abilities to discover some features of other animals' lives. Scientists still regularly make basic discoveries about familiar animals like dogs and pigs and cows. For this reason alone, some level of humility is in order.

We also know that some of the most prevalent ideas about certain animals are inaccurate. Certain caricatures of other animals dominated the past—many animals, such as wolves and orcas and gorillas, were thought of as extremely vicious and belligerent when in fact they are, in their own lives, quite different from how they have been portrayed. Another telling example from the past is the doubt that developed in some scientific and philosophical circles about whether other animals have consciousness or experience pain. Science has now provided abundant evidence suggesting many other-than-human beings have consciousness, pass classic tests of self-awareness, and have precisely the same pain mechanisms that we have.

As a bottom line, then, we can say that our species knows some impressive things about other animals. We can confidently state about *them* that (1) they are often different than we are, (2) some of them are very intelligent, live in complex societies, and have emotions, and (3) we have a great deal still to learn about virtually all of them.

Why do their realities matter?

There are multiple, common sense–based reasons for "getting it right" about other living beings' realities. In addition, there are many deeply personal reasons that different people have for seeking accuracy and clarity regarding the actual realities of other animals' lives.

A leading common sense–based reason for exploring other animals' realities, which is also a scientific one, is the pursuit of truth. Science since the seventeenth century has developed a collection of subfields that reflect our considerable abilities to inquire in disciplined and creative ways about the universe we share with countless other organisms and inorganic objects and systems. A standard goal in all these sciences is "the truth," which coincides perfectly with our natural curiosity. "Getting it right" about the realities around us also helps us have confidence in our ethical judgments about the world around us and its nonhuman creatures.

Another common sense–based reason for trying to learn about other animals is that humans have long recognized similarities between humans and many other living beings. Traditional sources, such as the Bible, the Qur'an, sacred writings from India and China, and the stories of indigenous peoples, often reflect the commonality attested to in the third chapter of Ecclesiastes (this translation is from the Revised Standard Version):

> For the fate of the sons of men and the fate of beasts is the same; as one dies, so dies the other. They all have the same breath, and man has no advantage over the beasts; for all is vanity. All go to one place; all are from the dust, and all turn to dust again. Who knows whether the spirit of man goes upward and the spirit of the beast goes down to the earth?

Science after science has confirmed these similarities. Many primates have a brain structure identical to that of humans, and humans have essentially the same arrangement of internal organs and bones as do chimpanzees, with whom we also share several important blood types. Humans and many other animals suffer from many of the same diseases. The fact that the pain mechanisms in many nonhuman animals are identical to those in humans suggests that some features of our experiences of pain overlap as well.

While for some it is controversial to suggest that other living beings have emotions at all like those of humans, the existence of emotions in other living beings has long seemed obvious to many people. Interestingly, scientists in the latter part of the nineteenth century were deeply interested in this question, but the science establishment of the early twentieth century indulged in a denial of other living beings' emotions, and this peculiar conclusion prevailed for much of the twentieth century. Chapter 9 discusses the late twentieth-century revolution wherein cognitive scientists pioneered a return to common sense on issues like consciousness, self-awareness, and emotions in other living beings. Science has recently detected certain kinds of cells in nonhuman brains that are thought to be the same cells that stimulate human emotions. Consider this December 2006 report that appeared in the widely circulated magazine *New Scientist*.

It turns out that humpback whales, fin whales, killer whales, and sperm whales possess spindle cells in the same area of their brains as spindle cells in human brains. This brain region is linked with social organization, empathy, intuition about the feelings of others, as well as rapid, gut reactions. Spindle cells, once thought to be unique to humans and other great apes, are believed to be important in processing emotions. And whales actually have more of them than humans do.

Because modern sciences have revealed startling genetic similarities between humans and some other animals (the percentages are always in the mid- to high nineties, but the different methods of comparison produce figures ranging from 93% to as high as 99%), the existence of behavioral similarities is to be expected.

Understandably, the features of other animals' realities that are similar to human experiences are often those that matter most to humans. In fact, for many who learn the basic facts about human/nonhuman similarities, it can be hard to understand the way that many important circles within the law, religion, science, and public policy deny them. In these realms, discussed at other points in this book, there are many people who remain adamantly opposed to admitting that other animals can be like humans in some fascinating respects. These circles have long been dominated by phrases like "humans and animals" because this way of speaking cements the idea of a radical difference between humans and other animals. The upshot is that our present ways of talking about other living beings often obscure the startling similarities that many humans have long recognized between themselves and other animals.

Some wings of modern science rely upon these similarities in practical ways. Some *nonhuman* animals are used in scientific experiments designed primarily to shed light on *human* realities. The scientist who wrote *Inside of a Dog* described an unlikely source of knowledge about humans.

> The behavior of rats in cages may be the single largest contributor to the corpus of psychological knowledge. In most cases, the rat itself is not of interest: the research isn't about rats per se. Surprisingly, it's about humans.... the millions of responses by millions of laboratory rats, *Rattus norvegicus*, have greatly informed our understanding of human psychology.

Note that the similarities that science underscores by using rats in this way, as well as many other animals that are far closer to humans in an evolutionary sense (such as primates), are not just physiological similarities. Countless experiments have been conducted on other animals' *psychological* dimensions in order to shed light on various aspects of humans' minds and personalities, such as addiction, the effects of maternal deprivation, and the biological basis of sharing. Chapter 3 quotes several philosophers regarding various ethical dilemmas that arise because of reliance on these similarities to investigate human problems.

Yet another common sense–based reason to seek out other animals' realities is that such knowledge is quite pertinent to how we treat them. We need to know other animals' realities in order to know the consequences of our actions toward them. Thus, if we are trying to help them survive and even if we are trying to minimize some harm to ourselves that we perceive them to bring to our human community, we need to know about their realities to know what actions to take toward them.

A final common sense–based reason to pursue accurate information about other animals' realities is that such knowledge will help us assess the heritage of claims about other living beings that we have received from our many human cultures. Is what we have been told about this or that animal correct, or is it inaccurate or somehow biased? Without good knowledge of other animals' realities, it is impossible to assess our ancestors' claims about the animals with which we share the world.

Apart from reasons anchored in common sense, there are also important personal dimensions of knowing other animals' realities. Personal curiosity, the aesthetic pleasure and even therapeutic benefits of watching wildlife or companion animals, the demands of moral compassion, relationship possibilities, and even spiritual connection—all of these have been advanced by innumerable people in every culture as reasons to "get it right" about other living beings.

How does science categorize animals?

The science of classifying living beings is most commonly called "taxonomy." Today it is also more technically known as "systematics" because the goal of this science is a systematic classification of living beings that reflects the evolutionary relationships among them. This attempt to arrange all living beings into related groups looks for common factors, which is possible today because of highly precise sciences like genetics. The basic classification scheme introduced by the Swedish botanist and zoologist Carl Linnaeus in the eighteenth century has been expanded to eight levels that now include *domain, kingdom, phylum* (in botany, *division*), *class, order, family, genus,* and *species.* This scheme tells us not only about general connections but also that the differences among living beings are more diverse than any culture ever imagined. This is because there are so many simple forms of life beyond the range of humans' eyes and ears and touch.

This is an important, even if rarely acknowledged, topic of animal rights because the overwhelming majority of life forms fall well short of what is normally meant when people use the word "animals." For example, the simplest forms of life are microscopic single-celled living creatures that scientists call "eubacteria" (*eu* is a Greek word that here means "true") and "cyanobacteria" or "blue-green algae." This invisible class of beings contains millions of different kinds of unicellular life that scientists refer to as the "Kingdom Monera." Scientists set these very simple, microscopic forms of life apart from other, altogether distinct "kingdoms" of living beings. Each of the other kingdoms (some schemes list four additional "kingdoms," while other schemes list five) contains almost countless additional forms of life. As important, each is a kingdom because its life forms comprise a dramatically distinct form of life.

Humans are members of the Kingdom Animalia, which has about one million different species. There are many living beings in this kingdom that we might call "animals" but which we often ignore when we talk about animal rights issues. Note as well that an important implication of the scientific classification of life into five different kingdoms is that the *vast* majority of living beings are *dramatically* different from the few tens of thousand species of living beings that humans are used to calling "animals." All vertebrates are in the Kingdom Animalia, but of the eight subdivisions of vertebrates notice how many (especially in the first four groupings) are unlikely to be included in animal protection petitions:

> Class Agnatha (jawless fishes); Class Placoderms (armored fishes); Class Chondrichthyes (cartilaginous fishes, such as sharks and rays); Class Osteichthyes (bony fishes); Class Amphibia (amphibians); Class Reptilia (reptiles); Class Aves (birds); and Class Mammalia (mammals)

At the back end of this list we finally arrive at mammals, birds, reptiles, and amphibians, which are the groups of animals that people have historically recognized. In particular, it is the community of mammals and, sometimes, birds (thanks to extraordinary beings like Alex the Grey Parrot) that many today argue on behalf of when promoting animal protection.

How valuable is this scientific map in animal rights discussions?

While the map of life created by scientists gives people in modern societies astonishingly detailed information about the kinds of life on Earth, a review of these general categories of life makes one feature of modern animal protection movements obvious—concerns for "animal rights" have, naturally enough, dealt with those animals we can see. Among those we can see, there occur many animals that are, like us, recognizable individuals. We can tell one dog from another, one cat from another, and so on. These can be thought of as the larger or *macro* animals.

Human cultures have divided these visible or macro animals in many different ways. Chapter 4 addresses various issues raised by cultural diversity in views of animals. Consider, though, how the Yolngu people of Australia describe the other animals in the world:

> *Living Creatures of the Salt and Fresh Water*
> * edible invertebrates, including shellfish, crustaceans, and larvae (except bee larvae), including molluscs and invertebrates with hands

- turtles, dugongs, and dolphins, including those with shells, those with twin-fluked tails such as whales
- stingrays and sharks
- fish, including freshwater fish and saltwater fish

Living Creatures of the Land
- bees and honey
- animals, birds, and reptiles, including flying animals (including bats) and small flying animals
- walking animals (includes the emu) and small walking animals
- crawling animals, including small crawling animals
- slithering animals (snakes) and small slithering animals

It is obvious *to us* that the Yolngu list is a limited list. It turns out that *any* land or even continent occupied by a certain tribe or people or industrial nation includes but a small percentage of the different forms of life. Because citizens in modern industrialized societies are the beneficiaries of globally shared knowledge about other living creatures, many of us recognize easily that the Yolngu classification scheme, or any other scheme of one locale's visible living beings, does not include all of the earth's animals.

Further, familiarity with a wide range of views of other animals and knowledge of the animals themselves together reveal that most humans are surprisingly uninformed about other living beings. This is most frequently due to the fact that only the narrowest range of other animals (of which most are "domesticated" or controlled by us) are part of our daily lives. Thus, even if we often know the names of animals and something about modern scientific classifications, we nonetheless know very little of what the named and categorized animals are like in their own free-living communities.

Beyond the level of our familiarity with recognizable individuals, there are two other significant problems. The vast majority of macro animals, that is, the animals visible to us, are *not* easily recognized as individuals. We generally cannot tell one sparrow from another or even one squirrel from another. We can become much better at this exercise if we try (there are some helpful clues in books like Len Howard's 1953 *Birds as Individuals*). But no matter how much we improve our native abilities to tell one living being from another, there remain many animals that we can see but simply cannot distinguish from one another.

Further, as the scientific listing of life reveals, there is an unbelievably vast and diverse universe of *micro* animals that are so small that we cannot see them at all. Add to this the multiple billions of microorganisms that exist on the surface of each person's skin and in our guts, and the world of living beings is rich indeed.

Consider one way in which this overview of the scientific mapping of all animals illuminates important features of the language used in the modern animal rights movement. That movement includes various advocates who regularly use inclusive language suggesting that humans should have concern for "all animals." This claim is by no means new, for one can find this claim often in the ancient civilizations of India, China, and the Middle East, as well as in many small-scale or indigenous societies around the world. This is one of the reasons that respected figures like Gandhi, Francis of Assisi, and Albert Schweitzer often used inclusive language of this sort.

Nonetheless, given that science reveals that so much of "life" is micro, or inaccessible to humans, claims about humans protecting "all animals" or "all life" need to be understood in context. Otherwise, they will seem a serious overstatement, because the goal of protecting "all animals" is, it turns out, no simple matter. For all practical purposes, the focus of animal protectionists from ancient times until today has been macro forms of life that we can easily identify. These include most mammals, some birds, and certain reptiles like turtles, but often not fish and certainly not many of the micro forms that are impossible to notice without the aid of a microscope or other technology. The invisible forms of life that science has been so diligent in identifying may constantly surround us, but we simply are not the kind of beings who can factor protecting them into our daily lives. Importantly, there are indications in our daily language that we take this into account, for while talk about killing animals is so morally charged that it regularly elicits challenges, talk about "killing germs" or using antibiotics (literally, "against life") does not.

How valuable are nonscientific categories when classifying animals?

The division of animals into macro and micro groups is, of course, an artificial division framed in terms of humans' abilities to notice others and take them seriously. There are many other division schemes used regarding the life we live amid—these include sacred and profane beasts, edible and nonedible creatures, clean and unclean animals. These categorization schemes are also based on human perception, preferences, and needs.

In modern industrialized societies, the division of animals into artificial groups also plays important roles. At times, these artificial categories become so familiar that some people think these divisions are the order of nature, created by some divinity for humans' personal use.

Since talk about other living beings and, especially, traditions of animal protection are about macro animals, it helps to examine some of the most familiar categories used by humans for different animals. Keep in mind that these categories are most characteristically defined *in relation to humans* and thus have little to do with the animals themselves. Some animals, such as dogs, horses, and pigs, appear in many of these familiar categories—all have been considered companion animals, research animals, food/production animals, and wildlife. This fact alone makes it particularly obvious that the categories discussed below (companion, research, entertainment, food, work, production, and wildlife) are constructed by humans for human purposes.

What do we know about the numbers of animals in existence?

While we can only make rough estimates of the number of animals in the different categories described below, it is a valuable exercise for several different reasons. It is illuminating to compare the human population, estimated by the World Bank and the United States Census Bureau to be just short of 7 billion as of the end of 2009, to the number of nonhumans generally and also to the number of animals in the popular categories described below. From these relative numbers, one gains valuable perspectives on the different ways in which humans are controlling some nonhuman populations.

Importantly, population estimates of many forms of life in this country or on that continent offered by expert and lay groups alike are mere guesses. Our uncertainty at this level is multiplied a hundredfold as we try to guess numbers of living beings worldwide.

Our uncertainty about populations is as true of macro animals as it is of micro animals. We do have good estimates of certain animals that are endangered (so we know that there are only a few hundred of this or that species), but for many animals the numbers given are simply best guesses rather than precise numbers. Addressing the population numbers for nonhuman animals is, revealingly, a humbling exercise.

But it is still natural to want to know the size of the population being discussed. In addition, the sheer size of some of the categories of animals addressed below, especially as they can be compared and related to human population numbers, helps us understand any number of things. These numbers help explain, for example, why there is considerable interest in some calls for change even as there is strong resistance to calls for changes in other areas.

Who, what are companion animals?

This group of animals is addressed first because today the companion animal category is extremely popular around the world. As chapter 5 mentions, legal developments regarding companion animals are impacting how humans think of all nonhuman animals in general. This is due to the fact that human interactions with our designated "companion animals" have taken on very special features in the last century.

The category "companion animals" is an example of the non-natural kind of category that sociologists and philosophers call a "constructed" category because the animals are grouped together because of their relationship to humans, not because of their inherent qualities. This category is thus elastic—not only might animals found in this category be found in other categories (such as food or research animals), but if a new kind of animal becomes a popular pet, then people will begin to speak of that new kind of animal as falling within this important category. In a very real sense, humans are also companion animals, but the term is typically used for dogs, cats, some birds and primates, and even some unusual mammals and other "exotic" animals (discussed at the end of this chapter).

One might think that numbers in this category are relatively easy to estimate because this is such a treasured and familiar category. But the numbers remain surprisingly elusive. Many governments do not collect census data on these animals. Neither is much information available on the precise number of companion animals killed simply for want of a home. We know that the number of unwanted dogs and cats killed in the United States, for example, has decreased dramatically, but it still exceeds several million annually because shelters regularly take the life of healthy and adoptable cats and dogs that they deem unadoptable due to a curable illness or a correctable behavioral problem, or simply because a shelter needs to make room for new entrants.

Best estimates of the number of companion animals in the country with the highest companion animal population (United States) include figures in the range of 70 to 90 million owned cats and 60 to 70 million owned dogs. Not included in these already vague figures are feral dogs and cats, which some estimates put as high as an additional 100 million animals (cats make up the majority of these). China is the only country with cat numbers approaching those of the United States. Estimates for China range around 45 to 60 million cats, while the pet dog numbers in China are about one-third as high.

Other countries with large numbers of owned cats (that is, not counting feral or unowned animals) include Russia and Brazil (10 to 15 million), and Italy, France, Britain, Ukraine, Japan, and Germany (7–10 million). The number of owned dogs in Brazil (in the range of 30 million) is twice the number of owned cats. Japan and South Africa also have more owned dogs (as many as 13 million in Japan and about 10 million in South Africa) than owned cats. Russia has fewer dogs (10 million) than cats, while France has about the same number of dogs (8 million) as cats. Poland and Thailand have high dog populations (about 7 million each). In Central America, South America (outside of Brazil), and Southeast Asia, the numbers are not well known, in part because many areas have high percentages of non-owned animals that roam communities freely.

In some countries, birds are popular companion animals. China has by far the most (perhaps 70 million), while Japan and the United States have as many as 20 million owned birds. Brazil, Indonesia, and Italy have from 13 to 17 million owned birds, while Turkey, Spain, Australia, and France each have from 6 to 9 million.

Such vagueness in national and regional numbers translates into especially vague numbers worldwide. The World Society for the Protection of Animals has reported in the past that "globally, there are some 600 million dogs, and a similar number of cats, of which an estimated 80% are stray or unwanted." Added to this rough number of cats and dogs must be the necessarily vague numbers for other companion animals—these include several hundred million birds, several tens of millions of owned horses, and tens of millions of turtles, ferrets, pigs, and other less common "companion animals." These numbers together can be used to suggest a total companion animal population around the world in the range of 1.5 billion.

Another indicator of concern for companion animals is the amount of money spent. In the United States alone, in excess of $40 billion is spent annually on pet food and products. If that number equals the amount spent in all other countries combined, companion animals are responsible for expenditures somewhere in the range of $100 billion worldwide.

Lavishing such extraordinary amounts of attention and dollars on nonhuman companions is a new phenomenon, but giving attention to certain nonhuman animals is not entirely new. In some cultures, there is archeological evidence indicating special relationships with one type of animal or another. In ancient Egypt, cat mummies were buried in staggering numbers—*National Geographic* reported in its November 2009 issue that after a mass grave of mummified cats was discovered in 1888, the volume of bodies was so great that they were sold for fertilizer, with one ship alone hauling more than 180,000 mummies to be spread on the fields of England. This story contains some ironies—it begins with cats so valuable at one period that they were mummified, and then ends with these cats' bodies, centuries later, being used as fertilizer in another country known for its animal sensibilities. In this way, the story helps one see that one era's valuation of certain animals can be quite different from that found in another era and another place.

The social bond between dogs and people is particularly ancient and widespread, with the *Journal of Archaeological Science* in February 2006 describing the "consistent and worldwide distribution" of the practice of burying dogs "over about the past 12,000–14,000 years." The article suggests this phenomenon reflects "how people often have responded to the deaths of individual dogs much as they usually respond to the death of a family member."

The quality and length of humans' relationships with companion animals of one sort or another reveal why the category of companion animals is important in animal rights discussions. Citizens in modern society stand in a long line of fascination with companion animals, which explains why this particular category has for decades now been luring vast numbers of people into animal protection concerns. As discussed in the law section, this category of animals is driving many important legal changes around the world. Concerns for companion animals have in many places reconnected people with concern for nonhuman animals in general, and this is now having many repercussions for the larger populations of food animals and wildlife. This is an important trend, for, as will be shown shortly, the population of companion animals is dwarfed by the astronomical number of food animals now raised and slaughtered.

Which animals are research animals, and how are they treated?

Many different species are used in a variety of scientific research efforts. Rats and mice account for as much as 90% of the animals used in major research countries like the United States. Estimates regarding the number of research animals used annually around the world always mention their own imprecision, because only about 20% of countries require detailed reporting of this use of animals. Further, of those that do require some reporting, exemptions for extremely important categories exist. For example, such is the case in the United States, where the use of rats and mice is excluded from the federal law reporting requirements.

The general estimates for this category are in the range of 100–200 million—in 2008 the Hadwen Trust and British Union Against Vivisection published an estimate in the journal *Alternatives to Laboratory Animals* suggesting that 115 million animals are used annually around the world in laboratory experiments. The University of British Columbia's respected Animal Welfare Program was less specific when it suggested on its Web site in 2009, "The total number of animals used globally in research each year is currently unknown, but it is likely to be in the hundreds of millions."

More exact numbers are available for some types of animals than others. The number of dogs used annually is known to be well in excess of 130,000 worldwide (estimated at approximately 140,000 by the Hadwen Trust study), because in the United States alone the number of dogs used annually is reported by government agencies to be in the 60–70,000 range. The Hadwen Trust also estimated that researchers use at least 35,000 cats, almost 90,000 primates, and over one million rabbits.

Historically, this has long been an area of tremendous debate. Today, the debate continues—some countries have made reduction in numbers an official policy following the 1959 proposal by British researchers Russell and Burch known as "the 3 Rs" (replacement, reduction, and refinement) in their landmark publication, *The Principles of Humane Experimental Technique.* Following the formal enactment of such policies, significant reductions in numbers have been reported. In 1994, the prestigious journal *Nature* cited a report from Tufts University that claimed the number of animals had been reduced between 20% and 50% in Europe since the 1970s, and by about 25% in the United States since 1985.

The decreases have not been fully consistent, and in a number of years within the last decade there have been record increases in the overall numbers of animals used. For example, the British government reported in 2009 a 14% increase in the number of medical experiments involving animals, the largest rise since modern records began. Thus, while the official government policy remains "replacement, reduction, and refinement," a few scientists in Britain have called for abandonment of this policy because they predict that more animal research, not less, will be required for adequate investigation of models of genetic disease.

Besides the most commonly used animals (rats and mice), the list of animal species used in research includes not only the dogs, cats, and primates already mentioned but also well-known animals such as guinea pigs, hamsters, sheep, and ferrets. Many unfamiliar animals, including horseshoe crabs, zebra fish, and fruit flies, are heavily used in highly specialized research.

Some pro-research groups point out that the use of valued animals such as dogs, cats, and primates is minimal, with these three groups accounting for less than 1% of all the animals used in research. Because the number of animals used annually is so high, the argument is invariably made in terms of percentage rather than absolute numbers—the 1% figure sounds low, but the realities are that several hundred thousand dogs, cats, and primates are used per year around the world. Such numbers often surprise companion animal advocates who have fought to protect dogs and cats in particular.

Numbers given above do not always include all of the testing done on animals regarding the safety of ordinary consumer products. In addition, the figures do not always reflect the now common phenomenon of genetic engineering, which is increasing and yet already around the world involves tens of millions of animals. (One company, for example, reported that it alone destroyed in excess of two million mice per year.)

Numbers in the range of 100–200 million animals annually for research worldwide may seem large, but the fact that the estimate is couched in the low hundreds of *millions* means the number of animals used in this category is relatively small compared to the *billions* involved in the other major categories. This is important from an animal protection perspective because in some ways, as noted in chapter 5, contemporary law as it applies to this category is so detailed as to make this category the most highly regulated area of human-animal interaction. The presence of detailed regulations, however, does not mean that this area is without its problems and suffering, for as scientists and nonscientists alike admit, suffering surely occurs and is inconsistently policed by both government and nongovernment organizations.

In fact, the legal terrain regarding research animals is quite complicated in some countries—one well-known example involves legislation passed in 1966 by the federal government in the United States that came to be known as the Animal Welfare Act. Although this legislation promised oversight of warm-blooded research animals, after the legislation was passed government administrators were able to minimize protections in an odd way. On their own, they overrode the plain meaning of the law and ruled that the law *excluded* rats, mice, and birds, all of which clearly fit into the category of warm-blooded animals. This ruling was allowed to stand for more than a decade, even though the law itself clearly did not call for this exclusion. Eventually, after decades of wrangling over this exclusion led to a tentative settlement whereby rats, mice, and birds would be covered, the United States Congress reacted by amending the law to make the exclusion permanent.

This story has another complicated twist. Even though the Congress made the exclusion of rats, mice, and birds permanent, voluntary reporting by many institutions beyond the technical requirements of the law provides additional possibilities of protection and oversight. The situation of research animal protections today in many countries continues to be complicated, with no shortage of reports of inconsistent enforcement and even outright failure to put certain laws into effect.

What is the situation with entertainment animals?

The category of "entertainment animals" includes nonhuman animals trained to perform, fight, and even kill for humans' enjoyment. Included are animals on exhibition in circuses, movies, racing, and many forms of fighting. Zoos are sometimes included in this term as well.

Uses of animals for entertainment raise animal protection issues because taking animals out of their natural community and environment is almost always harmful to them. Even more harmful is prompting them to perform actions that are not part of their natural lifestyle and normal behavioral repertoire.

Additional issues arise because most animals used for entertainment purposes are subjected to living and training conditions that involve harsh practices. For example, elephants, tigers, chimpanzees, and dolphins in captivity are typically compelled to become submissive to a trainer, and those that are used for performance are treated in ways that prompt many protectionists to object. Undercover videos have repeatedly shown that some animals used for entertainment are continually maltreated throughout their performance years in an effort to make them behave on cue when in public. Since the training of these animals takes place prior to their public appearances, the harshness of the pre-appearance training may not be evident during performances, and the difficulty of proving cruelty during training on inaccessible private property makes denials of mistreatment easy. A number of law cases have been brought to successful conclusions after undercover video revealed harsh practices.

The historic roots of animal entertainment go deep. Imitation of nonhuman animals is widely thought to have played a role in the origin of human music and dance, and early musical instruments were often made from animal parts and shaped like various animals. Exhibition of animals, which takes this connection a step further, dates back to at least the third millennium B.C.E. and occurred in a wide variety of places, including ancient Egypt, China, Mesopotamia, Greece, and Mexico.

The most notorious exhibition of animals in the ancient world took place in Rome, where animals were held for slaughter on a regular basis. Augustus recorded the slaughter of as many as 3,500 African animals, mostly lions and leopards, in one series of events. This number pales in comparison to the 11,000 animals slaughtered in a series of games staged by Trajan a century later. Collecting and holding animals continued into medieval times in European and Asian centers, and eventually developed into the more modern notion of municipal zoos, of which the London Zoological Garden, founded in 1826, was the first claimed to be an explicitly scientific institution. (Chapter 7 has more on zoos.)

Entertainment animals are often associated with the long-standing tradition of circuses, which are increasingly subject to legal restrictions and even bans (examples are given in chapter 6). Some traditional entertainment practices, such as fox hunting and bull and bear baiting, have now been outlawed in many places. Dog fighting and cockfighting have also been formally banned in many places, but both remain common as underground practices. Traditions such as dancing bears and use of monkeys and apes to lure tourists have been discouraged in many places, but bullfighting, rodeos, and dog racing continue to thrive despite some local attempts to curtail these traditions.

Horse racing continues to be widely accepted despite high-profile deaths in recent years. It is difficult to deny when one is next to a modern racehorse that the individual animal has beauty, grace, and power. Yet many inside and outside the horse racing industry are aware that some of the humans who own racehorses are far less concerned with the animals' welfare than with winning at all costs.

The use of nonhuman animals in films has in some countries been the subject of both government legislation and voluntary restrictions in the form of industry-enforced codes. But such regulation applies in only some countries, and then often only regarding treatment of the animals while the movie is being filmed. Any cruelties that take place outside that limited time frame are not typically covered by industry-enforced codes.

Because the entertainment industry covers such a wide range of animal uses, it has produced very diverse examples of animal use and abuse. Since entertainment is a luxury, uses of nonhuman animals in this manner are characterized by many critics as the least justifiable of contemporary animal uses. But defenders of the use of animals in entertainment have been successful because such uses involve privately owned animals whose work is profitable for the human owners. Laws that govern the right to use private property as one wishes can thus be used to shield abuses of entertainment animals.

What is the status of animals used for food?

Today there is renewed debate over food animals in many societies. The debate is often complicated and contentious, for there is much at stake. Much that is said in other parts of this book relates to food animals, such as the story in chapter 5 where an American lawyer refers to chickens as no more important than manure and trash.

One set of contributors to the debate includes individuals and companies invested in farm animals. Some of the claims of this group are astonishing, and give one reason to wonder if Upton Sinclair's adage that "it is difficult to get a man to understand something when his salary depends upon his *not* understanding it" is particularly true in the industrial circles where farm animals are owned. Consider an example taken from the book by George W. Bush's speechwriter. The passage describes a conversation the author had with the president of the largest pork producer in the United States during a tour of modern production facilities. The animals being talked about are pigs kept for their *entire* lives indoors.

> I ask, isn't there something, you know, just a little sad about locking millions of animals away like that?
> "They love it," Sonny (Faison) replies.
> "They do?"

"Yeah, they don't mind at all.... The conditions that we keep these animals in are much more humane than when they were out in the field.... the healthier, and [more] content the animal, the better it grows. So we're very interested in their well-being—up to an extent."

There are prominent voices that disagree vehemently with the corporate president's self-serving claim that pigs "love" such conditions. The following passage is taken from the 2006 best seller *The Omnivore's Dilemma* by Michael Pollan.

Piglets in these CAFOs [a U.S. government term that means "confined animal feeding operations"] are weaned from their mothers ten days after birth (compared with thirteen weeks in nature) because they gain weight faster on their drug-fortified feed than on sow's milk. But this premature weaning leaves the pigs with a lifelong craving to suck and chew, a need they gratify in confinement by biting the tail of the animal in front of them. A normal pig would fight off his molester, but a demoralized pig has stopped caring. "Learned helplessness" is the psychological term, and it's not uncommon in CAFOs, where tens of thousands of hogs spend their entire lives ignorant of earth or straw or sunshine, crowded together beneath a metal roof standing on metal slats suspended over a septic tank. It's not surprising that an animal as intelligent as a pig would get depressed under these circumstances, and a depressed pig will allow his tail to be chewed on to the point of infection. Since treating sick pigs is not economically efficient, these underperforming production units are typically clubbed to death on the spot.

An institutional voice on problems in the treatment of farm animals appears in a 2008 report published jointly by the Pew Charitable Trusts and the Johns Hopkins School of Public Health. The report states straightforwardly, "By most measures, confined animal production systems in common use today fall short of current ethical and societal standards."

Such differences are hard to resolve in today's atmosphere of polarized debate. Those who challenge harsh practices are labeled animal rights activists or worse (for example, the Humane Society of the United States has been called by some a "terrorist" organization). On the other side, those who work in food industries are called monsters or worse.

Consumers today have considerable power to impact the outcome of the polarized debate, for consumers can choose among meat and non-meat alternatives. Even when one chooses to eat meat, citizens of both industrialized and developing countries can seek options such as locally produced meat that avoid the worst problems of industrialized meat production systems.

Meat remains a staple for the majority of people who can afford it, and while many different animals are eaten by humans, the vast majority are chickens, fish, pigs, and cattle. Other animals widely recognized as being heavily used for food include ducks, turkeys, goats, sheep, rabbits, and many shellfish. Here the discussion focuses on the principal three types of land animals eaten (chickens, pigs, and cattle), although a number of very important practical and ethical points could be made about animal protection concerns directed at many other kinds of food animals as well.

As the quoted passages above suggest, modern food production processes involving pigs raise ethical issues for a number of reasons. This is also true of the production processes that govern chicken, cattle, and many other "farmed" animals. Some of the problems are caused by the sheer volume, for the numbers involved in modern food production are startlingly high. Between 50 to 100 *billion* animals are slaughtered every year for food. A large majority of these today are chicken, hogs, and cattle.

Some food animals, such as milk cows, might not be thought of as meat animals, but they are important sources of meat in several ways. After short lives as production animals (they live only three to five years of their 20-year life spans), milk cows are shipped to the slaughterhouse to become hamburger. Further, during their production life, they are kept pregnant in order to produce milk, and they give birth after nine months or so. The female offspring eventually replace their mothers when the latter are shipped to the slaughterhouse. The male calves become veal, which is one category of farm animal practice that has received an enormous amount of attention because the calves are given such an impoverished life after being taken from their mothers only days after birth.

Many industrialized nations today employ the modern processes known generally as factory farming. The United States is a leader in this approach, and the American government agency responsible for inspections (the Department of Agriculture) publishes *daily* slaughter figures that are revealing of the scale of factory farming today. The "Estimated Daily Livestock Slaughter under Federal Inspection" for November 11, 2009, *alone* included 122,000 cattle, 433,000 pigs, 10,000 sheep, and 3,000 veal (male) calves. The daily figures for chickens are not published, but the *one-day* figure if published would have been in the range of 27,000,000 (based on an annual slaughter number of 10 billion chickens in the United States alone). The number of animals killed in this category is multiples of 10 times greater than the combined number of companion animals and research animals. As the largest of the human-centered categories, the population of food animals is rivaled in size only by wildlife numbers.

Fish have not been mentioned here, of course, and since, as pointed out in chapter 2, most living beings are not vertebrates but instead micro animals, there still are many living beings besides fish not accounted for in the story told here.

The bottom line is that, from the vantage point of even the simplest forms of animal protection, let alone the robust protections often associated with the notion of animal rights, food traditions are complex terrain to traverse. Because food animal production is massive, complex, and new, it has raised many ethical issues that are by no means simple to resolve. As one moves from issues centering on the treatment of animals to other issues with important ecological dimensions, and from those problems to the dangers faced by slaughterhouse workers, the topic of food animals appears to be plagued by ethical issues piled upon ethical issues.

The treatment of the animals themselves is obviously an issue that has classic animal rights dimensions. The mistreatment of food animals to be slaughtered is an ancient theme, for as noted in chapter 6, religious traditions originated humane rules about animal sacrifice. In the western tradition, many sources have lamented the harsh treatment of farm animals. No passage is more famous than the following from Upton Sinclair's classic 1906 novel *The Jungle*, where one finds a reference to "rights" combined with our irrepressible concern for the suffering of individual animals:

> It was all so very businesslike...porkmaking by machinery, porkmaking by applied mathematics. And yet somehow the most matter-of-fact person could not help thinking of the hogs; they were so innocent, they came so very trustingly; and they were so very human in their protests—and so perfectly within their *rights!* They had done nothing to deserve it.... Was it permitted to believe that there was nowhere upon the earth, or above the earth, a heaven for hogs, where they were requited for all this suffering?

Does factory farming pose environmental risks?

While the treatment of the animals is the dominant animal rights issue in contemporary debates, ecological issues also play an important role today in debates about factory farming because pollution from food animals is astonishingly serious. The United Nations division known as the FAO (Food and

Agriculture Organization) issued a 2006 report titled "Livestock's Long Shadow." In the words of this report's executive summary, livestock production facilities are "probably the largest sectoral source of water pollution, contributing to eutrophication, 'dead' zones in coast areas, degradation of coral reefs, human health problems, emergence of antibiotic resistance, and many others. The major sources of pollution are animal wastes, antibiotics and hormones, chemicals from tanneries, fertilizers and pesticides used for feed crops, and sediments from eroded pastures."

Although figures for the whole globe are not available, this FAO report indicates that in the largest consumer economy (the United States) "livestock are responsible for an estimated 55% of erosion and sediment, 37% of pesticide use, 50% of antibiotic use, and a third of the loads of nitrogen and phosphorus into freshwater sources." Similarly dire figures and their consequences for the human community can be found in the Pew/ Johns Hopkins joint report, which concluded, "Furthermore, the concentrated animal waste and associated possible contaminants from [intensive] systems pose a substantial environmental problem for air quality, surface and subsurface water quality, and the health of workers, neighboring residents, and the general public."

What other sorts of risks does factory farming pose?

Beyond the ecological problems that compromise both human communities and other-than-human communities, there are further causes for concern connected with factory farming. For example, the dangers faced by slaughterhouse workers are among the greatest of any industry. In her 1997 book *Slaughterhouse*, Gail Eisnitz was able to talk as much about the harms to humans as to nonhumans. Eisnitz's subtitle, *The Shocking Story of Greed, Neglect, and Inhumane Treatment inside the U.S. Meat Industry*, turns out to be as much or more about the harms to humans as it is about the multiple out-of-view harms that are the essence of modern mega-production of meat and dairy products.

There are also other risks *for humans alone* in modern production, which has often been promoted because it produces cheap food. The human risks, not the nonhuman problems, were the overwhelming focus of Eric Schlosser's 2001 best-selling *Fast Food Nation: The Dark Side of the All-American Meal* and Pollan's *The Omnivore's Dilemma*.

As discussed in chapter 6, the jobs of many human workers can be at risk when animal rights proponents seek to change the worst features of industrialized production of food. But when the joint 2008 report from Pew and Johns Hopkins examined the economic contribution of factory farming to communities, its conclusion was blunt—"the *costs* to rural America have been *significant.*" The report explained its reasoning.

> Although many rural communities embraced industrial farming as a source of much-needed economic development, the results have often been the reverse. Communities with greater concentrations of industrial farming operations have experienced higher levels of unemployment and increased poverty.... Associated social concerns—from elevated crime and teen pregnancy rates to increased numbers of itinerant laborers—are problematic in many communities and place greater demands on public services.

A further layer of losses is suffered by communities because factory farms, through their sheer size, outcompete family-owned farms. The 2008 report thus adds, "The economic multiplier of local revenue generated by a corporate-owned farming operation is substantially lower than that of a locally owned operation. Reduced civic participation rates, higher levels of stress, and other less tangible impacts have all been associated with high concentrations of industrial farm production."

Food issues are, as pointed out in the chapter 6 discussion about national and ethnic food traditions, characteristically very important in cultures. This means that questions about a particular food tradition or practice will very likely be perceived as encroaching upon the right of people to pursue their own cultural tradition. Long-standing uses of animals also have many additional psychological and economic anchors. Chapters 6 and 7 address the related issues of the political and social dimensions of the animal rights debate.

More than tradition is at issue, however, when considering the place and treatment of food animals in human society. Dramatic increases in the number of factory-farmed animals have changed production realities, such that long-standing husbandry traditions have been abandoned. Husbandry has been replaced by a preoccupation with economic efficiencies and "production parameters." It is this way of thinking that has licensed talk of the kind described in chapter 5 where living beings are equated to trash and manure.

The fact that industrialized animal farming abandons not only husbandry traditions but also impacts local communities negatively in economic and environmental terms gives many citizens a range of reasons to oppose factory farming, even if they choose to continue eating meat by seeking out locally raised meat. European nations have shown interest in the "dignity" of farm animals, and some North American producers have, following consumer pressure, agreed to phase out one practice or another (for example, gestation crates for pigs). But many practices continue unchallenged, and factory farming is expanding around the world today in response to estimates that meat consumption in the developing nations will double over the next two decades.

What about work and production animals?

"Work" and "production" by nonhuman animals are human-centered terms that encompass an extremely wide range of uses. Beyond the "work" that food animals, entertainment animals, and companion animals do for humans, there is much other, less well-known "work" and "production" that an astonishing variety of animals provide for the human community. The classic image in western culture is the horse pulling any variety of vehicles, while in eastern cultures the dominant images are elephants and horses as transportation or war machines and oxen pulling plows and carts.

The treatment of work animals has been a source of much ethical concern in the western cultural tradition—this category played an important role in the development of both social and legal awareness, since the first animals given legal protections in the modern era were working farm animals. The 1822 legislation in England popularly known as Martin's Act listed "ox, cow, heifer, steer, sheep, or other cattle" (but, interestingly, it was held not to include bulls). The classic 1877 novel *Black Beauty* by the English author Anna Sewell, which is told from the horse's point of view, broke new literary ground and spawned many other accounts written in the voice of non-human animals. Sewell wrote the book as an attempt to, in her own words, "induce kindness, sympathy, and an understanding treatment of horses." In the last chapter of the book, Sewell added, "There is no religion without love, and people may talk as much as they like about their religion, but if it does not teach them to be good and kind to other animals as well as humans, it is all a sham." The novel had a very powerful impact on the public and it, along with much other literature modeled on it, increased concern greatly for not only the welfare of work animals but for dogs as well.

Not all of the work done by nonhuman animals is as harsh as that memorialized by the *Black Beauty* story. Some work animals are considered partners, even family members. The work they perform ranges from herding to carrying heavy loads. American Indian tribes used dogs for a variety of purposes before horses were introduced to North America by the Spanish in the eighteenth century. Service dogs today perform an even wider range of tasks, from sniffing out bombs, drugs, and cancer to helping children with reading.

The therapeutic uses of nonhuman animals for the benefit of humans reveals how astonishingly versatile domesticated animal partners can be.

Other working animals have received much renown—pigs have long searched for truffles, messenger pigeons once plied the skies with essential human communications, and hunting dogs continue to be bred and sold in great numbers. Such uses can cause harms, for our history with work and production animals clearly shows that when we use other animals as mere resources whose value is measured in terms of benefits accruing solely to humans, some humans insist on total domination and protection of human interests alone. For example, hundreds of millions of animals are slaughtered for fashion purposes (fur and leather). Thus, it is common for one to hear calls for changes, even abolition, of this practice or that involved with work and production animals.

Because the working relationship between humans and certain other animals has been an enduring relationship, it has the status of a traditional cultural icon in many places. This strongly suggests that working relationships are clearly going to continue.

Many other animals are held for production of medicine-related products. A particularly flagrant example is the East Asian tradition of caging bears for the production of bile. Many activists within China now challenge this practice (chapter 10 includes an example). Most commonly, conditions for production animals are set up to maximize production, not cater in any way to the animals' needs. But sometimes conditions are unique—this is the case with the quarter million horseshoe crabs used to produce a substance that keeps surgical implants, pacemakers, prosthetic devices, and other items free of bacteria. Manufacturers spend $50 million a year on this substance, drawn from live crabs. The crabs are returned to the wild, and most survive. There is relatively little activism directed to this practice, while the challenges to true luxuries such as fur have been profoundly widespread and effective.

Is today's widespread concern for food and production animals new?

While it is true that polls, publications, and the focus of non-profit organizations in a number of countries reflect a surge in animal protection concerns regarding food and production animals, the concern is not new, but instead a renewal of a long-standing tradition (with roots in religion) that has been subordinated in many of the industrialized nations of the world.

The surge in modern interest in farm animal protections is reflected in a 2004 poll conducted by Ohio State University, which is located in the heart of an area known as the Farm Belt. The survey of this state's socially and politically conservative, farm-oriented public revealed that an astonishingly high number (92%) agreed or strongly agreed that it is important that farm animals are well cared for. An almost equal number (85%) had the opinion that the quality of life for farm animals is important even when they are used for meat. Eighty-one percent also agreed that "the well-being of farm animals is just as important as the well-being of pets," and 75% agreed that "farm animals should be protected from feeling physical pain."

These concerns, especially when they are tied to calls for change, are sometimes labeled "animal rights." Since these welfare-oriented concerns do not challenge the propriety of killing the animals but only the ethical issues raised by mistreating them on the way to their death, they provide an example of concerns for the moral rights of living beings, but such concerns fall short of classic examples of animal rights where any serious harms to other animals are condemned.

A close examination of concerns for farm animals suggests that they are a combination of at least three separate trends. One trend is reflected in polls—animal protection has drawn increasing interest in many countries around the world. Concern for food animals is one area where this is being worked out. Another trend is reaction to the harshness and harms of modern production methods. While the Ohio poll numbers affirm that these moral dimensions cannot be avoided when humans use other living beings as food, the high percentages also reflect concerns for environmental and public health problems. The report of the UN agency FAO cited in this chapter also identified factory farming as a major source of global warming (greater even than the transportation sector). Further, factory farming has also produced significant public health problems like obesity, as documented in best-selling books like *The Omnivore's Dilemma* and *Fast Food Nation.*

Some of these problems—such as obesity, the emission of greenhouse gases, and economics-driven production methods that ignore moral issues like killing and mistreatment—are new challenges. Traditional uses of animals for food and work—that is, uses of nonhuman animals before the introduction of technological fixes like the use of antibiotics—were premised on a special relationship or husbandry contract. This relationship has features that in many societies provide important shields for the nonhuman animals involved.

Traditional animal husbandry features what amounts to a kind of bargain or contract that creates for humans both benefits and responsibilities to the animals. The animals raised under a husbandry contract benefit in one sense—they are provided protection and fed. An example familiar to citizens in western culture is the Psalm 23 image: "the Lord is my shepherd, I shall not want." To be sure, husbandry is *not* primarily a compassion-based story—the driving feature is better understood as utilitarian in the sense of, "We take care of them, and they take care of us." If a farmer violated this husbandry compact, the punishment was immediate—the bargain was lost, for the animals did not provide because they died.

Modern industrialized production, because it is driven solely by economic efficiencies and not the practicalities of the husbandry bargain, violates the husbandry ethic because technology (such as the heavy use of antibiotics) allows factory farmers to crowd living animals into facilities. The suffering of the animals is irrelevant as long as the production methods produce sufficient profits.

In this way, modern factory farming techniques override concerns for other living beings as sentient animals that suffer when they are mistreated as mere resources, even "trash" as the lawyer story in chapter 5 attests. This insensitivity to the suffering of other living beings is, as noted in chapters 6 and 7, one of the reasons that food animal issues have come to the fore in many countries.

The role of modern veterinary medicine in such forms of technology, including the field of "animal science" described in chapter 9, is of great concern to many practicing veterinarians and others concerned with animal protection. The pages of the American profession's official journal (*Journal of the American Veterinary Medical Association*) regularly contain complaints by veterinarians about the complicity of organized veterinary medicine's leadership in industrialized approaches to food and production animals. The American professional organization is particularly dominated by industry-oriented values, and this has caused the profession's leadership to issue many position statements that oppose legal changes that offer additional pro- tections to not only food animals but also to research animals, wildlife, and even to companion animals and their owners.

Who, what are wildlife?

This final category is unlike the other categories in one important respect—the category of wildlife is, by definition, composed of animals living free of human domination. "Wild" or free-living animals are defined by a natural norm, not uses of these animals for the human community. Nonetheless, wildlife is hardly free of human impacts. Destruction and pollution of habitat, the presence of human-generated diseases, disruptions caused by invasive species introduced by humans, and many more "anthropogenic" (or originating with humans) harms impact free-living animal populations greatly.

This category is crucial for any number of reasons—five are identified here, but many more could be advanced. The first has already been underscored—those animals who live free of direct human domination contribute to our understanding of life's complexities. They feature communities that nurture complex social realities and individual-to-individual relationships, as well as distinctive forms of intelligence, personality, communication, emotions, and so much else that is beyond what we as humans can experience on our own. In very important ways, wildlife can enrich humans in ways that humans cannot enrich themselves.

A related reason for this category's importance is that wild animals have long been an important ethical and spiritual resource for humans. Many of our cultural resources attest to this important feature of wildlife in its natural world. Shakespeare observed, "One touch of nature makes the while world kin," and Henry David Thoreau suggested that "in Wildness is the preservation of the World."

Not all views of wildlife have been so positive. In ancient times, although many cultures held respectful views of some wild animals, there were also negative views of wild animals and wilderness in general. The influential Philo of Alexandria, a Hellenized Jewish philosopher born in Egypt, imagined in the first century C. E. that wild animals were *continuously at war* with humans, and that their "hatred is directed...towards ... mankind as a whole and endures...without bound and limit of time."

Today, though, wildlife provides, as it always has, a test of the human spirit. Richard Louv's 2005 best seller, *Last Child in the Woods*, the subtitle of which is the hopeful *Saving Our Children from Nature-Deficit Disorder*, calls out a risk to children that many parents and educators have not perceived well. Louv describes the multiple ways that children are removed from the more-than-human world and the corresponding disadvantages suffered by children because of impaired development of their rich cognitive and ethical abilities.

> For a new generation, nature is more abstraction than
> reality....Our society is teaching young people to avoid
> direct experience in nature. That lesson is delivered in
> schools, families, even organizations devoted to the out-
> doors, and codified into the legal and regulatory struc-
> tures of many of our communities....Yet, at the very
> moment that the bond is breaking between the young
> and the natural world, a growing body of research links
> our mental, physical, and spiritual health directly to our
> association with nature—in positive ways.

Wildlife poses a most basic question to us—what will we leave
for our children and their children?

A third reason that the wildlife category is important is that
many habitat and population problems already exist for
free-living populations, and many more are coming. The tra-
jectory of habitat destruction, the expanding problem of alien
or invasive species altering ecosystems, the tragedy of species
extinction, and the problem of emerging and reemerging diseases moving from humans to wildlife and vice versa are such
that these problems will not soon be solved.

Challenges on the horizon also include a range of problems
associated with global warming, as well as the pronounced tendency of governments concerned with public health threats to
focus on elimination of nonhuman populations and communities in order to minimize threats to humans. Further, there are
extremely serious enforcement problems with laws "on the
books" (that is, laws already enacted). These laws may nominally protect wildlife, but often they are not enforced. In 2005,
according to Interpol, the world's largest police organization,
crimes of illegal hunting and trade in wildlife were, in dollar
volume, second only to drug trafficking. Complicating matters
greatly is the problem of rich hunters from industrialized,
affluent countries plundering poor countries' wildlife—Scully
in his influential *Dominion* includes a revealing chapter on
Safari Club International members who in their own country

are "law and order" supporters but nonetheless willfully violate other countries' prohibitions on wildlife hunting.

A fourth reason to be concerned about wildlife revolves around wildlife population questions. This number is not at all easy to estimate because of the sheer diversity of life. Another difficulty is human dominance, which makes other animals shy of human presence and depletes wild animal populations. As noted earlier, humans and their domesticated animals completely dominate other, free-living vertebrates on land. Further, an uncountable number of living beings are not vertebrates. Yet in light of the fact that the vast majority of these are invisible to humans, they do not have any real presence in the daily lives of human individuals. They are thus not factors in the modern animal protection movement.

Humans quite naturally are interested in animals that, like themselves, have interesting personalities, lifestyles, and communications. These "charismatic megafauna" include the wildlife groups that have drawn the most attention from the animal protection movement—whales and dolphins, elephants, the nonhuman great apes and primates in general, and a number of causes célèbres like rhinos, tigers, whooping cranes, and condors.

A fifth reason wildlife is so important to our human community is addressed in the following section—this is the argument that wildlife provides a better window into nonhuman animals' realities generally than does familiarity with companion animals.

It is important to know that historically attitudes toward wildlife have changed again and again, thus providing a good example of how attitudes toward other animals is a matter of human choice. Very ancient views saw many animals as justifiably to be feared; but many wild animals were also seen as relations, guardians, bringers of blessings, even as divinities. These ancient attitudes have been supplanted by dismissive, negative attitudes toward nonhuman animals in many circles of the modern world. The result has been the slaughter of the wildlife native to Europe, North America, and so many other places.

The prevalence of negative views in industrialized countries softened during the nineteenth century, such that wildlife is often now romanticized and again thought of as bringers of blessings. Because in recent years many countries have significantly revised their existing legislation or adopted new legal frameworks for the protection and management of wildlife, this area provides a good example of the ongoing ferment in human/nonhuman relationships. Domestic legislation and international wildlife treaties reflect new strategies for protecting biodiversity and decreasing threats to wildlife both inside and outside protected areas. One tool used is better understanding of social and cultural dimensions of wildlife management, which includes involving local people and stakeholders in decision making.

There are still some views of wildlife that are decidedly negative, however. Many agriculture-based veterinarians today understand wildlife not as noble creatures that might thrive alongside the human community but as reservoirs of disease. Public policy can be very dismissive of wildlife in such circumstances, even though most of the public and certainly the majority of veterinarians clearly see wildlife as patients, not as vermin or threats to domesticated animals. Tensions between views of wildlife as valuable in and of itself and views of wildlife as competitors and even threats to humans remain to be resolved.

Are wild animals more truly "animal" than are companion, food, production, and research animals?

One issue for informed citizens to consider when thinking about "animal rights" is, *which animals* deserve *which protections?* Animal rights approaches have always been limited as a practical matter to those animals that humans can easily notice and thus not to the vast majority of living beings. Companion animals are the darlings of many today, but by definition they are within, usually under, the influence of humans. Using companion animals as the measure of "animals" is thus risky, for companion animals are possibly subject to the distorting features of the natural subordination and submissiveness to humans that were essential to their domestication. Free-living animals do not have these features. So it is natural to ask, does this freedom make them *more animal*, as it were?

If humans can notice and take seriously only some of the earth's myriad animals, or if it turns out that only some non-human living beings can be protected by humans as we seek to help our human community thrive, which ones should receive which protections? Humans easily reach the conclusion that those disease-causing microorganisms with which humans cannot coexist should be minimized. But which beings should we promote? Is there any reasonable argument that we, as moral beings, can eliminate other living beings simply because we consider them unappealing or noxious? What does a moral being do in such situations?

Today, as elaborated in chapter 5, most discussions about animal rights focus on companion animals. Nonetheless, many people still unreflectively assume that "wild animals" are the *true* animals, thus rationalizing our human dominance over food, research, companion, work, production, and entertainment animals. As noted above, there is some plausibility in claiming that wild animals are a particularly enlightening form of nonhuman life when it comes to knowing what animals' realities actually are.

But even if familiarity with free-living nonhuman animals is the best framework from which to understand what nonhuman animals are *really* like, we still have to ask how helpful the distinction between "wild" and "domesticated" is when it comes to animal rights. Are wild or free-living animals, on the one hand, and domesticated animals on the other, different in important respects for the purpose of fundamental protections? If human control impacts domesticated animals, changing their realities and possibilities, why would that make them any less worthy of protection? Domesticated animals are individuals in each and every way that free-living animals are individuals, and they are similarly sentient beings capable of a wide range of experiences and suffering. Since these animals are under human control, there is an additional reason for morality-minded humans to take responsibility for not harming them.

There remains the important insight that wildlife presents unique opportunities to understand the possibilities of life out beyond our species line. Wild animals demonstrate intelligence, communication, personalities, emotions, sensory abilities, and other features that have long commanded many humans' respect. But these are also traits of many domesticated animals. When humans experience such complexities beyond our own species, paradoxically such experiences push humans to become as *fully human* as we can be, that is, human in the context of a biologically rich world full of other interesting living beings.

The special bond that develops between humans and their companion animals surely opens a unique door to the companion animals' realities—we live with them and thus experience them regularly in ways that we could never experience wild living creatures. Research animals are a different matter, for although they often win the heart of people in the laboratory setting, they are in the end being used as mere tools. Food animals are a complex proposition—subsistence hunting is natural, but factory farming is not. In fact, as already noted, industrialized farming creates dire problems for both the nonhumans *and* the human communities in which it exists. A comment made by Bernard Rollin, Colorado State University's emeritus professor in philosophy and veterinary medicine, who has been the leading veterinary ethicist in the world for the last three decades, is particularly revealing.

> One of my colleagues, a cow-calf cattle specialist, says that the worst thing that ever happened to his department

was betokened by the name change from Animal Husbandry to Animal Science. No husbandry person would ever dream of feeding sheep meal, poultry waste, or cement dust to cattle, but such "innovations" are entailed by an industrial/efficiency mind-set.

One can fairly ask what happens to other animals' spirit when we cause them to be born, and then imprisoned for their entire lives, in factory farms. One should also ask, what happens to our own spirit when industry leaders, policy makers, and educators claim that no moral issues at all are at stake in such practices?

What other categories are popular?

There are many additional categories into which we place other animals. Here we consider some of the most common ones, but new categories will surely be developed even as others are modified and perhaps even become obscure.

"Exotic animals" is a term used by ordinary people to convey that the animal is from an unusual species. Under the law, though, this can be a specialized term that refers to animals that are not native to a particular area (hence, "exotic animals" in a state or province will be those that are introduced, rather than those that occur naturally in that state or province).

Another prominent constructed category is "circus animals." Since circuses are changing, with the most successful providing more human acts and far fewer nonhuman acts (because they are being banned from many cities and even whole countries), this category may eventually fall into disuse.

The movement of humans from continent to continent results in the shifting of nonhuman animals and plants as well. Thus, the term "invasive animals" is common in the modern world. Many of these have supplanted native species, and there is great controversy over how to respond to this serious ecological risk.

The terms "pest" and "vermin" remain part of everyday language. But today there is much more awareness that human interests are not the only ones that we, as moral beings, can notice and take seriously. As a result, many more people recognize that dismissive terms of this kind have limited usefulness.

"Dangerous animals" is both a commonsense notion and a significant legal term. In law, a person who brings an inherently dangerous animal into the human community can have strict liability (that is, liability for any and all harms), no matter how carefully managed the animal was before it caused harm. Dogs can also be labeled "dangerous" when they have bitten someone or the owner has reason to believe they might bite someone.

"Totem animals" and "sacred animals" have played a very important role in humans' understanding of their relationship to the more-than-human world. A totem animal is one understood to be either kin or somehow otherwise incorporated into a family-like relationship with one's tribe. Sacred animals have existed in many societies for many reasons—for example, as already noted, ancient peoples all over the world once held positive views of other animals.

Another familiar category from religious traditions is the idea of "clean and unclean animals." The latter often are connected to taboos about touching or being near the animal (dead or alive). The notion that a particular kind of animal is disgusting is present in almost all known human cultures, and several well-known religions have this as a prominent category. In the Jewish and Islamic traditions, there are very prominent dietary laws found in the tradition's most fundamental scriptures that govern what a believer can and cannot consume. Additionally, mere contact with some animals is at times thought of as unclean—for example, in some Islamic cultures dogs are viewed as causing impurity, but today there are signs that this is changing in some Islamic circles.

"Imaginary animals" have little to do with animal rights, but some scholars who work in fields like "literature and animals" or "religion and animals" spend much more time talking about this category than about the biological animals that occupy the earth with humans.

"Therapy animals" have received much attention in recent decades, although the calming effect of other animals has long been known. Today, scientific research has opened up many new vistas into what is variously called animal assisted therapy, animal assisted intervention, and animal assisted activity. Some national laws require that such animals be given access to public places and otherwise protected, although the policy behind such protection focuses on the human receiving therapeutic help, not the nonhuman animal. Many different kinds of animals can fall into this category, the best known of which are dogs, cats, horses, and dolphins. Many other animals can have demonstrable calming effects on people, including elephants, birds, rabbits, guinea pigs, and fish.

Because we often shape these and other categories to reflect human priorities, the future is likely to bring new categories. Existing categories will possibly evolve, as has happened over time with companion animals. The new category of "transgenic animals" has precedents—humans have been shaping domesticated animals through selective breeding for centuries. But the novelty of creating new animals by directly altering genetic materials reveals that humans' control over the other-than-human beings with which we share the earth has reached a new level. Whether this new ability produces entirely new categories of living beings is a very sensitive matter for a variety of reasons. Some people find this the deepest of ethical issues. Others dislike the God-like features of creating new forms of life. Still others fear the effects of creating new forms of life without really understanding the risks—this is sometimes referred to as the Frankenstein syndrome. Whether this new and profound ability to change life is handled in an ethically sensitive manner or proceeds merely in terms of the property rights of "owners" of the technology and animals remains to be seen.

3

PHILOSOPHICAL ARGUMENTS

Here we turn to some important distinctions that everyone needs to know. These distinctions can become very technical and academic if one wishes to go that way, but the basic issues are relatively easy to understand. This chapter starts with the key distinction between moral rights and legal rights. To understand why this is an important beginning point, it helps to know that key claims about "rights" both inside and outside the animal rights debate often rely on vague and inadequate definitions of what rights are (this is discussed further in chapter 5). If one tries to use a poorly thought out idea of rights for *other animals*, especially in the face of ignorance about the animals involved, the result is like blowing smoke into fog-clarity is not enhanced.

Clarity is, for many reasons, very desirable in this area. Some of the less-than-clear thinking about animal rights is promoted by those who oppose rights of any kind for nonhumans, while some of the sloppy thinking is promoted by those who claim that rights are the solution to every problem humans cause nonhuman animals. Some opponents of animal rights are fond of misdefining "animal rights" as "a philosophy that animals have the same rights as people" (see the glossary). Since humans rights are rich and diverse, and include civil, economic, political, social, and cultural rights, it makes little sense to claim than anyone seeks to give other-than-human animals "the same rights" that people now have. It is true, without question, that honoring rights for other animals diminishes some existing human privileges—this issue is dealt with more fully in chapters 5 and 6.

Animal rights advocates also make claims that confuse what is at issue. As already mentioned, the claim that "all animals" should have rights sounds beautiful, and such broad claims have long been made by religious and nonreligious figures alike. But this claim needs to be unpacked carefully. In addition, claims like "all animals are equal" and "all life should have equal rights" need to be scrutinized carefully if we are to communicate well about "rights" for living beings of any kind.

As George Orwell once observed in an essay titled "Politics and the English Language," our language "becomes ugly and inaccurate because our thoughts are foolish, but the slovenliness of our language makes it easier for us to have foolish thoughts." Some may think Orwell unduly harsh, but his description unfortunately fits many discussions of rights. It is important that Orwell explained his motive in the following sentence—"the point is that the process is reversible." In fact, any educated, intelligent person has the ability to refrain from the mistakes that have plagued vague and even lazy uses of the concept of rights. Such problems have constantly caused people talking about "rights" to talk past one another, and this has to date been especially true when the topic is rights for nonhuman animals.

The confusion is reversible *if* we take time to ask what the speaker means when he or she uses "rights." In particular, what any of us means when we talk of "rights" will be clarified by the use of a number of helpful adjectives. We begin with the important distinction between *moral* and *legal* rights.

How do moral *rights* differ from legal *rights?*

A technically correct answer to the question about the difference between moral rights and legal rights sounds simple at first—moral rights are anchored in a system of morality, while each and every legal right is anchored in a specific legal system. This answer is only a start, however, for there are two problems lurking in the background that make this technical-sounding answer far too simple. These problems stem from the fact that we have inherited two very different traditions of talking about "rights." Each is very important today, but because they perform different functions, keeping them distinct is critically important if the goal is to talk to, not past, one another.

The first problem is that many people assume that legal rights are always moral rights. If this were the case, making the "legal versus moral" distinction would not be so crucial. But the relationship of law with morality is not nearly this simple. Some laws have a direct connection to morality, as with laws against murder. But other laws have nothing at all to do with morality, like rules about which side of the road we drive on.

Even more revealing is that many important laws that have been passed are later repudiated as fundamentally and irrevocably immoral. Examples are unfortunately easy to find—they include laws supporting slavery or those barring people of one race from voting or marrying members of other races.

We all know there is *some* connection between law in general and public morality, if only because legal systems need public support or the social order will break down. Law, then, clearly has some features that are like morality's features, especially since the rule of law can create order in a society, and that alone makes it function like social values or ethics. This is why some philosophers see the foundations of law in morality. For example, animal rights philosopher Tom Regan made this observation in the 2001 book *The Animal Rights Debate:*

> The framers of America's Declaration of Independence...
> maintained that the sole reason for having a government
> in the first place is to protect citizens in possession of
> their rights, rights that, because they are independent
> of, and more basic than legal rights, have the status of
> moral rights.

But even if it is common for people to understand law in a democratic society to have some relationship to morality, there remain many laws that either have nothing to do with public morality or, worse, are immoral because they benefit some small group and harm the larger human community. Laws that powerful people put in place to harm less powerful people—which in the nineteenth and twentieth centuries prompted liberation movements that sought more democracy, more freedom for ordinary people, more equality for women—are not at all moral, but merely backed by force.

It is thus misleading to claim that *all* laws and legal rights are based in morality. This is why it is helpful to identify those "rights" that are morality-based, as opposed to those rights that are based in a specific legal system. These may overlap at times, but as a practical and political matter these are very different animals that should be carefully distinguished.

This distinction is easy to remember if, with regard to legal rights, one keeps in mind that each and every legal right is anchored in a specific legal system. The legal system gives the different legal rights both specificity and authority. Moral rights, on the other hand, draw their strength from something other than law. Their source or foundation is not a legal system but instead a different kind of human tool or system we call "morals," "morality," "ethics," or even "cultural values." So even though, as pointed out in chapter 5, legal systems are quite diverse, they *all* identify legal protections with a high degree of specificity. They characteristically work on definitions and argument. The result is that those special protections we call "legal rights" are called out in some public document like a constitution, statute book, or court record, and this gives the legal rights specificity and authority.

This first problem that arises because many people assume that legal rights are always moral rights can be solved easily enough *if* we are conscientious about using the adjectives "legal" and "moral" to clarify what kind of claims we want to make.

But a second problem lurks in the background, and it arises because of some peculiarities in the notion of "moral rights." These peculiarities grow out of the fact that, unlike legal rights, moral rights are not called out with any degree of specificity in a particular place. This means they often are vague, sometimes maddeningly so. And it also means that the authority behind moral rights is less specific than is the authority behind legal rights. The upshot is that claims about moral rights can be manipulated in different ways, and they can mask some less-than-moral motives, such as selfishness, bias, oppression, or even dishonesty.

There are a number of reasons for the imprecision so characteristic of claims about moral rights. One is the diversity of moral systems available to any person—it turns out, there are lots of competing, often mutually exclusive moral systems that claim to be the basis for moral rights. Each religion teaches its believers moral values, and the claims of different religions compete with each other and with secular worldviews. When one religion claims that its morality is based in one set of revealed scriptures, another religion counters with its own revealed scriptures.

Similarly, each secular morality has its explanation, which may anchor explanations of moral rights in naturalism, nationalism, racism, or some other ism. Since different secular moralities justify their claims about moral rights in different ways, and since religions use their own specialized approaches to morality, there is little chance of any objective process of determining which moral system is right.

So if we hear someone claim, "this being has a moral right," we will better understand what is at issue if we take the time to identify the underlying moral system that is the foundation for this claim. Some moral systems have been very narrow, protecting only property-owning, free white males, while others have protected only the people of one tribe or race or nation. The most famous moral systems these days are those associated with populous religions like Christianity or Islam or

Hinduism or Buddhism or the Chinese traditions, and each of these gives a different explanation of why certain protections are *moral* rights. Every person interested in morality eventually must confront a simple, bedrock fact: each moral system calls out its own set of "moral rights" and justifies these rights in its own peculiar way.

We can say generally, though, that today most moral systems nominally include all or at least most of the members of the human species. Many of these moral systems go beyond the species line. They do this to different extents and in a variety of ways. Some communities, such as those in the Indian subcontinent (for example, the Jain community), have built a reputation on their wide-ranging commitments to protecting different beings beyond the species line as much as possible. Others have anticruelty protections but not much else. Collectively, our moral and ethical systems reveal that extension of moral protections beyond the species line has been common.

So when someone says this being or that being deserves *moral rights*, we need to ask further questions about the values of the underlying moral system in order to get a clear understanding of precisely what is being claimed. When this is done, and especially when the adjectives "legal" and "moral" are applied to talk about "rights," the slovenliness Orwell complained of is, as he himself suggested, reversible. There will no doubt still be differences, but at the very least people will be talking to, rather than past, each other about these differences.

What role has philosophy played in the modern animal rights movement?

The animal protection movement is one of the areas where *academic* philosophy has played an important role in today's society. "Academic philosophy" refers to subjects that are taught traditionally in academic centers like universities and colleges, and also a variety of approaches to ethics, reasoning, and some traditional philosophical questions found in academic books and journals.

Philosophers have helped in particular with the problems that arise when the discussion of rights is centered on moral rights. Peter Singer and Tom Regan have provided widely read explanations of why protection of other animals is a moral matter. Other philosophers have worked to provide accessible explanations of moral rights—claims about "natural rights" or some general category like "the rights of man" may be common and seem somewhat specific, but the forcefulness of these claims is undercut by the vagueness of the claims. Philosophers and others point out regularly that, as a practical matter, people have often been pressed to know what such claims mean and thus how to enforce them. As one travels around the world, one finds that there is no consensus on which moral rights are "natural" or "universal" for all humans.

Unlike the case with legal rights (where there is a court or legislature available to define words, give examples, and otherwise set some boundaries), there is no single and final authority that clarifies such questions about moral rights. Thus, when someone claims that moral rights are natural— that is, that they are not made by humans but are found or discovered or revealed—philosophers have worked to clarify what this might mean. Accordingly, claims about natural rights have been subject to much criticism, a famous example of which comes from the philosopher Jeremy Bentham, who referred to such claims as "nonsense upon stilts." Bentham understood both moral and legal rights to be a product of human agreement. Such human-made rights are called *positive* rights because humans *posit* them, that is, put them in place.

Debates about natural versus positive rights still occur, and the distinction plays a role in some discussions of animal rights, since many people feel that the obligation to treat other living beings well is not merely up to humans but is instead mandated by a moral code that humans are not free to alter.

Yet notice one implication of the legal-versus-moral rights distinction that philosophers have helped clarify—*however one answers the deep questions* that drive debates about whether natural rights exist at all (everyone agrees that some positive rights exist), it is clearly the case that *humans can recognize the relevance of talk about "rights" to both human and nonhuman living beings*. This is true no matter how one anchors those rights (that is, whether they are natural or positive rights, or whether the discussion is secular or religious). Greater clarity will exist in any debate if judicious use of adjectives like "legal" and "moral" is practiced, and also when participants are able to talk to one another about whether they are claiming "natural rights" or merely human-made rights.

When participants are careful in this way, it is possible for all to recognize that even if there is disagreement on the source of rights, humans may nonetheless agree that respecting moral rights, however they are explained, is an important human responsibility to all kinds of living beings. Whether the humans who agree on moral rights in this way then move on to create specific legal rights or other legal protections is an important but separate question. With a combination of moral and legal rights, humans are clearly capable of protecting a wide variety of living beings.

Thus, although the term "rights" continues to be used in both different ways and in a bewildering variety of contexts, the term is now in play regarding nonhuman animals. This has meant two very important things. First, even with all the limiting factors identified by philosophers and others, and despite being plagued by vagueness and even the risk of someone cleverly dismissing such claims as nonsense upon stilts, talking about *moral rights* is a respected way of claiming that an individual of some species is important. Second, talking of moral rights has deep roots in many human cultures and thus provides a broadly respected way of talking that can complement the other principal way of talking about rights, namely, specific *legal* rights recognized within a specific legal system.

What have been the principal philosophical arguments about the moral importance of animals?

Given that a constant theme in *any* area involved in studying our fellow animals is the diversity of human thinking, it is to be expected that philosophical arguments addressing the moral importance of other animals feature a great deal of variety. The diversity of argument is in part related to the problems described above that stem from the sheer diversity of moral and philosophical systems that humans have developed.

The diversity of argument also stems from another fact—arguments have been advanced for *millennia* by so many different people in different cultures because every human culture has recognized that there is tension between using living beings as resources and protecting them as valuable in and of themselves. Variety in these arguments is also related to the different kind of animals that people have sought to protect. As noted in chapter 2, some animals are so simple that killing them seems to many people to raise no more problems than does killing plants. But some nonhuman animals are so obviously complex that killing them raises problems on the order of killing humans. The diversity seen in arguments about killing the most complex nonhumans is much like the diversity one sees in arguments about when it is justifiable to kill humans.

Regarding the *quality* of philosophical arguments about what we might do with and to nonhuman animals, the respected philosopher Bernard Rollin observed, "Most of the accepted views of animal ethics are not reasoned positions, however. They are prejudices, expressions of self-interest, or habit. As such, they rarely can be defended rationally."

Philosophers have paid particularly close attention to ethics-based arguments that have been advanced regarding the moral status of animals. In academic ethics, one common approach sorts out ethics-based arguments into three main divisions: utilitarian thinking, rights-based thinking, and virtue-based thinking. These divisions apply as fully to purely human problems as they do to nonhuman animal issues.

Such a three-part division is a simplification, for there are many other ways of thinking about ethics. For example, the divine commands found in a religious tradition's revealed scriptures provide a very popular way to assess what is moral when dealing with other living beings. Similarly, the feminist ethic of caring also provides an approach that is based not on mere thinking and calculating but instead on humans' considerable abilities to care about others.

Further, each of the three main divisions of philosophical ethics discussed below has many alternative versions. What follows is a series of generalizations or guidelines about these principal ways of thinking about the moral importance of other animals. Each of these theories has been advanced in subtle, context-sensitive ways that give these approaches a flexibility and power that the following generalizations might not suggest.

Utilitarianism focuses on whether an act produces, on balance, good or bad consequences. In essence, it is a philosophy that makes the promotion of happiness and the relief of suffering the determinative element of all moral choice. Utilitarianism is most often associated with the English philosopher Jeremy Bentham, but this form of philosophizing utilizes a form of reasoning or calculating that is employed by virtually every human each day in assessing what action to take. Bentham's contribution was to make utilitarian calculation of good effects versus bad effects the single principle by which we can deem an action moral or immoral.

Utilitarianism is important in animal rights discussions for two separate reasons. Although it was a philosophy directed primarily at human issues, it was the first form of modern western philosophy that took on the animal issue squarely. People have always been of the opinion that many other animals can suffer just as people do, but the philosophical approach called utilitarianism, from its origins in the eighteenth century, gave other animals permanent recognition in the western philosophical tradition and its discussion of the domain of morality. The most famous utilitarian quote about nonhuman animals is Bentham's observation, "The question is not, Can they *reason*? nor, Can they *talk*? but, Can they *suffer*?"

It is important to know that utilitarianism is *not* based on rights but on interests. It involves calculating which action advances the most interests the furthest. One result of this calculation-based approach is that the interests of one being can be overridden because doing so produces so much good for so many others.

For this reason, utilitarian-based morality is decidedly unlike morality prescribed by those ethical theories that start out from the notion of rights. Rights-based theories are often classed in a single group called "deontology" (from the Greek word *dei* meaning "it is right" or "it is necessary"). This is a form of ethics that stresses the absolute demand of duty in contrast to utilitarianism's calculating approach based on an assessment of good results versus bad ones. In a rights-based approach, the interests of the right holder are protected *no matter* how much good might result if one chose to override those rights. So for a deontologist, even if killing one right holder would save thousands of others, the life of the right holder cannot be taken, because such an act is wrong in and of itself. Preserving the one life thus becomes necessary, even though society and many other right holders will then suffer bad consequences.

This rights-based thinking is today a familiar form of reasoning and is the basis on which virtually all modern societies hold that human beings cannot be used in experiments unless they give informed consent. Other rules given absolute status by some famous deontologists include acts that fall far short of ugly, repulsive acts like killing a human being—a famous example is "never lie." The shortcomings of deontology can appear when one considers such a rule, for lying sometimes produces extraordinarily important results (as when the police of an evil tyrant knock at your door and then ask if you are hiding any people of a disfavored ethnic group—if you lie, the members of the oppressed group you are hiding will live; *but if you must tell the truth no matter what the consequences,* innocent people die unnecessarily at the hands of the evil tyrant). In this fact scenario, the constraints that deontology puts on doing good seem mysterious to many, for it is not obvious why the constraint to tell the truth must be so absolute.

As different as utilitarianism and deontology are, both are used today in ways that harm other animals. Utilitarian thinking and its cost-benefit calculus are characteristically worked out by humans in ways biased toward human interests, such that the interests of the nonhuman animals end up completely subordinated even when relatively minor human benefits (like furs or other luxury consumer products) are at stake. Deontology is often framed as if only members of the human species are right holders, and thus other animals end up completely outside the circle of beings that are protected by this form of ethics.

Interestingly, both of these approaches have animal-friendly forms. As already mentioned, utilitarianism from its inception recognized that the interests of animals had to be part of any calculation that took suffering and happiness seriously. Deontology has also been framed in ways that make killing nonhuman animals an act that is in and of itself immoral (unless, as is also the case with humans, self-defense of innocent people from an attacker is at issue).

Both of these forms of ethics presuppose that individual humans can take the viewpoint of other beings into account. Utilitarians have to figure out the harms suffered by each sentient being, and deontologists have to figure out who should be the right holders. Admittedly, calculations of these kinds done to date have been extremely biased in favor of humans, and it is a classic animal rights position to observe that biases for humans are often deeply unfair. Many religious traditions have agreed, holding that the beings deserving fundamental protections go beyond the human species—the famous *ahimsa* notion (also called the principle of no harm) that sits at the heart of many religions from India, which today provides protections for both humans and nonhumans alike, was originally a doctrine developed for nonhuman animal protections.

The third alternative in the trio of major ethical approaches is often referred to as "virtue ethics." This approach is based on the view that the foundation of morality needs to be development of a right way of living. Said another way, virtue ethics focuses on the development of good character traits, hence its name "virtue ethics." This view that a person is good if that person has virtues and lacks vices stems in the western moral tradition from Aristotle's approach to ethics. This ancient approach underscores that a connection to community must be part of how we talk about "ethics."

Proponents of virtue ethics suggest that other ethical theories focus too heavily on individual acts and thus fail to explain what it is that leads to a life of character. Because they are so concerned with character, virtue ethicists place special emphasis on moral education because virtuous character traits are developed in one's youth. While some virtue theorists mention as many as 100 virtuous character traits that contribute to making someone a good person, the most commonly cited virtues include courage, temperance, justice, prudence, fortitude, liberality, and truthfulness. Bad character traits or vices include cowardice, insensitivity, injustice, and vanity.

In summary, virtue theory is driven by the insight that virtue animates the ethical life, *not* employment of a single general calculating principle like utilitarianism uses and *not* the deontologist's slate of absolute rules for determining what act to perform in any and all situations. Rather, virtue ethics presents us with the question of what a person in wise balance would do in life amid community.

It should by this point be obvious that, in a general way, virtue theory could be quite compatible with care for nonhuman animals *if* the virtues emphasized are compassion-intensive. But this has not been the case in many societies, though it has been true in some (for example, many Buddhist societies, though not all). Aristotle, the founder of western virtue ethics, was very human-centered, and so theorists who are impressed with Aristotle do not generally analyze problems in a way that notices and takes seriously the nonhuman dimension.

A key insight that everyone should appreciate in discussing philosophical views regarding our obligation to other animals is that modern societies have not inherited a single tradition but, instead, a hodgepodge of conflicting fragments. We are followers of the deontologist Immanuel Kant and the utilitarian John Stuart Mill in respecting and affirming personal autonomy; we implement utilitarian values in other ways, too, such as when choosing who gets what in emergency situations; we honor Platonic ideals and perfectionism in various ways; we embrace the political values of John Locke when giving private property respect; and we follow religiously originated values when idealizing charity, compassion, equal moral worth, and the importance of humility.

A final key insight comes from the veterinary ethicist Rollin.

Clearly there are no differences between people and animals that can conceivably bear the weight of excluding animals from the scope of moral concern and from the full application to them of our moral notions. Not only are there no morally relevant differences, there are clear-cut morally relevant similarities.

What does philosophy suggest about our "knowledge" of other animals?

Two uncommon words are the focus of this section because they help one begin to resolve some of the issues mentioned in chapter 2. The first is the philosophical term "epistemology," and the second is the German word *Umwelt*.

A number of philosophers have denied that we can *know* with certainty a great deal about other animals' realities. This clearly conflicts with what many people feel they easily recognize regarding the realities of familiar animals—that they are conscious and even self-aware, suffer pain, think with intelligence, understand at least some of what we attempt to communicate to them, have emotions and personalities, and so on. Humans have for millennia been protecting other animals in a variety of ways based on our confidence that we do perceive them well enough to assess complexities in their lives, such as communication, intelligence, suffering, and other features that tell us who and what they are.

The challenges to knowledge one finds in philosophical discussions of epistemology (the study of knowledge itself) often have an element of common sense to them. For example, since we cannot know some things with absolute certainty, we cannot claim *knowledge* of those things. So on the issue of whether another *human being* has consciousness that is like ours, or whether that human being is telling us the truth when she says something like "I have a pain" or "I am depressed" (she could be deceiving us about her subjective experience), philosophers have suggested that we have to admit that our "knowledge" of such things is more of a guess than a true certainty. This same kind of reasoning is very relevant to "knowing" what is happening inside the lives and minds of nonhumans.

One reason this is particularly true of other animals is that, as already mentioned, lots of other animals have special abilities that humans do not have. On the basis of our own special but clearly limited set of abilities, we struggle to know what it is like to be that other kind of animal with its different abilities—a famous essay in philosophy by Thomas Nagel titled "What is it like to be a bat?" suggests that we are, in the end, very limited when it comes to knowing what life is like for altogether different kinds of beings.

It is helpful to know that one need not explore all of the technicalities and complications of this sort of philosophizing in order to appreciate the basic insight regarding the limits of what we, as humans, can know. Frankly, we already have plenty of reasons for humility—for example, we already know from our own life experiences that we often have to guess about many things in life because absolute certainty is a rare thing. So we make what amount to informed guesses. This feature of our life is quite important in every human endeavor from science to ethics. This point is relevant to our judgments about nonhuman animals, as is made clear in a very elegant way by the philosopher Daniel Dennett in his 1995 essay titled "Animal Consciousness: What Matters and Why."

> ...a curious asymmetry can be observed. We do not require absolute, Cartesian certainty that our fellow human beings are conscious—what we require is what is aptly called *moral* certainty. Can we not have the same moral certainty about the experiences of animals? I have not yet seen an argument by a philosopher to the effect that we cannot, with the aid of science, establish facts about animal minds with the same degree of moral certainty that satisfies us in the case of our own species.

Any number of philosophers have commented on this "curious asymmetry." James Rachels observed the following dilemma about attempts to use *nonhumans* in research in his 1991 book *Created from Animals: The Moral Implications of Darwinism.*

> In order to defend the usefulness of research [researchers] must emphasize the similarities between the animals and the humans, but in order to defend it ethically, they must emphasize the differences.

Bernard Rollin, upon considering this dilemma, made the following suggestion:

> From a strictly philosophical point of view, I think that we must draw a startling conclusion: If a certain sort of

research on human beings is considered to be immoral, a prima facie case exists for saying that such research is immoral when conducted on animals.

Whether one agrees with these philosophers about the details, the general point remains that we know other animals are often complicated in some way or another. We thus know they might suffer like we do, and we also know that we can, *if we choose*, protect them.

The second word considered here is *Umwelt*, which in German means "environment" or "surrounding world." The term was used creatively by Jakob Johann von Uexküll, a German biologist who was interested in how living beings experience the world. Uexküll recognized that each being perceived its local environment in highly subjective ways based on its limited sensory abilities. Flies negotiate the world with their compound eyes, so they see an object like a flower differently than does a dog, whose eyes are altogether different. Dogs' eyes are more like human eyes but register only black and white, even though humans see a greater variety of color in the flower. But humans do not experience nearly as much of the flower with their noses as do dogs.

Each being lives in its own *Umwelt*, that is, "self-world," which extends only as far as the limits of one's sensory abilities. Humans do not see infrared or ultraviolet light, magnetic waves or other parts of the real world that are simply beyond us but which are experienced by some other living beings. Humans do not have echolocation abilities, and thus have a difficult time gauging what whales, dolphins, and bats do with this ability. The limits on any living being's biological abilities impact not only what that being can experience but also what that being can communicate to others.

These self-world bubbles are natural, and while communicative and inventive humans have fascinating ways of getting beyond our own limits, we are only beginning to learn how to talk about other animals' different experiences and realities. As pointed out elsewhere in this volume, we know that many other animals have communication, personality, social connections, and even emotions. But we have often simply assumed these realities away.

An important animal rights theme is that we, in our modern societies, have been *so* concerned with human realities, often talking as if the world was designed for us, that we have deprecated what other animals experience and do in their own lives. We talk ardently about discovering life on other planets, even though we remain immature in our thinking about other living beings' lives. We have been *so* self-interested that we have failed to use our imagination to explore *their* realities as they live and play in the more-than-human world we share with them. The notion of *Umwelt* is but one of the ways that creative, careful thinkers have tried to convey that other living beings' realities are different than our human realities. We still have much to learn about how such notions can help us in our attempts to sort out what it is that we can know of *their* worlds.

4

HISTORY AND CULTURE

The history of humans interacting with the living beings outside our own species is deep and broad. Any single attempt to tell the whole story of how humans have seen and reacted to, as well as protected or harmed, our fellow Earth creatures is bound to be partial. No one version of the story could possibly encompass the astonishing diversity of human cultures and the integral role that thinking about and treating nonhuman animals has played in countless human lives. Add to this already complex picture the unfathomable diversity of life from continent to continent and ecosystem to ecosystem, and the task of framing an adequate picture of this remarkable history is among the greatest of human challenges.

We can begin the story by asking some basic questions that will help us see the outlines of what we now know of this story, which in turn will suggest to us various things that we need to learn. For example, it makes sense to ask what options might have been available to a group of humans who, looking about their world, wanted to feel that they *really* understood the lives of the nonhuman animals that shared their ecological niche. They might have asked such questions for practical reasons, such as hunting for food, or they might have wanted to learn about other living beings for ethical or spiritual reasons—all of these concerns appear regularly in our past. Subsequent sections of this book address specific topics like law and science, but equally important are both the broad cultural approaches to protecting other living beings and the intensely personal responses one sees in the realms of ethics and religion, each of which comes up again and again in any number of this book's parts.

We can also ask how the options chosen by different cultures compare to the options now available to us as we survey the world in which we live. Each person is born into a particular culture that already carries a preexisting set of views of surrounding life. As mentioned in chapter 2, members of any particular culture or nation are *always* heirs to perspectives on animals that have their limitations. Some individuals in that culture may add to or modify this heritage somewhat, but the larger picture passed on to coming generations is likely to contain a great deal of traditional lore about other living beings.

Sometimes modern historians tell the story of human interaction with other living beings in very stilted ways, as when they tell the story as if it took place primarily within western culture. This approach is sometimes taken out of ignorance of the fact that other traditions have a different story, and sometimes out of the conviction that the story within the western cultural tradition is the version of the story that really matters because, for a variety of reasons, this cultural tradition has turned out to be the most important tradition to those listening to the story.

Another reason some historians tell a stilted, narrow version of the human-animal story is their impression that in the last 35 years, more impassioned pleading on behalf of other living beings has taken place than took place in the previous 2,000 years. This claim is only partially right—there has been a remarkable upsurge in concern about nonhuman animals in western countries in the last decades. But the claim that today's ferment is unique ignores much history in a wide range of cultures where concerns for animal rights have been long-standing and deep.

Telling the story in a narrow way is misleading for many other reasons as well, not the least of which is the sheer richness and diversity of views outside the western cultural tradition. A fuller alternative is to present views that include the perspectives of other peoples, such as various North American Indians, South American natives, Pacific Islanders, East Asian peoples, Sub-Saharan African cultures, Islamic communities, South Asian civilizations, Australian aboriginal groups, and indigenous European societies whose story did not make it into the mainline story of western culture.

The point here is simple—no one culture catches all of the issues and nuances of humans' possibilities with other living beings. That story is rich beyond belief, and the modern animal protection movement has only begun to tap this diversity.

When did animal protection first occur?

There has been no time in recorded history when respect and concern for some nonhuman animals was not an element in the human story. Indications from prehistory, that is, the time before we have any records, are that animal protection, in the sense of respect for the living beings themselves, reaches back to time immemorial. The researchers who have pieced this background information together suggest that our ancestors often thought of living beings as messengers from the divine, sometimes even as divinities themselves. Spiritual connections of humans to other, nonhuman lives were simply assumed, and humans deemed themselves one community among others.

In the parts of recorded history that lead most directly to western cultural traditions, the story is more complicated. There were animal-friendly views among the ancient Hebrews and Greeks, but each of these formative cultures for the western tradition also promoted views that, in different ways, emphasized the importance of humans over other animals. In the early centuries of the Common Era (that is, from the first few centuries after Jesus lived), the human-centered aspects of these two cultural sources combined. By the time of the death of Augustine of Hippo (in the early fifth century), the mainline institutions of the Christian church, which then dominated the governments of western culture, promoted what seems to modern minds and hearts a comprehensive dismissal of other animals. There were, however, always subtraditions that were more sympathetic to other living beings. (One well-known example is Francis of Assisi, but there were literally thousands of other Christians before and after Francis who were extremely animal friendly.)

As western culture moved into and through the Middle Ages, the Renaissance, the Reformation, the Age of Discovery and the conquest of what has come to be called the "New World,"the Industrial Revolution, and on into the twentieth century and beyond, animal-friendly views always existed. Another good example is the work of Albert Schweitzer (mentioned in chapter 10). It is true, however, that animal-friendly views were often subordinated to a version of the human-animal story that suggested that the earth had been made for humans.

This one part of the larger story is mentioned here because today it is often told as if it is the whole story. But the whole story of human-animal interactions both within and *outside* the western cultural tradition is rich beyond belief, and today it is part of the heritage of all peoples.

Does animal protection occur in all cultures?

In several important senses, the answer to this common question is a resounding yes. First, *every* culture has featured some version of the anticruelty ethic. Second, every culture and every religion has included many individuals who discovered that connections to other living beings were an integral part of their spiritual life and development. Not all religious institutions advance this insight, but at least some religious believers from every tradition have come to this conclusion.

It helps to know that animal protection has historical and cultural backgrounds of great breadth and depth. With such information, one understands better why every ethical system has taken humans' relationship to other living beings into account in some manner or another. It also helps one recognize that today's animal rights movement is a continuation of a deep heritage that has, in important ways, been forgotten in industrialized societies.

The insight that humans' moral abilities carry over to other living beings has, however, been interpreted at times in very self-serving ways. What has been considered cruel in one place and time has varied greatly. For example, many of the practices that have emerged as part of the modern phenomenon called factory farming (discussed in chapter 2), such as confinement and early separation of offspring from the mother, would have been deemed per se cruelty by our own grandparents and their forebears.

In a very real sense, then, today's animal rights movement has features that are direct responses to the fact that in modern societies the important heritage of anticruelty has been challenged as never before. This is one of the driving forces behind the comment of the presidential speechwriter Scully quoted in chapter 1 about no prior age ever having "inflicted upon animals such massive punishments with such complete disregard." The specific target of Scully's comment was industrialized or factory farming, but he could well have been speaking of any number of wildlife, research animal, and companion animal problems around the world.

Has there been an increase in the number of people protecting animals?

There has been an increase in two different senses. The first is the less important sense—the human population itself has increased so much that there are many more people alive today who engage our long-standing human tradition of animal protection. While this development does mean that there are more volunteers available for the animal protection movement, the increase in the size of the human population has spinoff effects like increased pollution, development pressures that cause habitat loss, and increased production of the gases that cause global warming (all of which are very harmful to other animals in a variety of ways).

There is another, stronger sense in which there has been an increase in the number of people concerned with animal protection. Many surveys reflect what the poll about farm animal welfare cited in chapter 2 reveals, namely, that as time passes a greater percentage in the public acknowledges the importance of animal protection.

A related phenomenon is the spread of animal protection concerns around the globe. There are now many groups in South America, the Middle East, Eastern Europe and Russia, and the Far East that work on animal issues as effectively as do the better known groups in Western Europe, Africa, Australia, New Zealand, and North America. Internet-based listings of animal protection groups have increased dramatically—for example, the World Animal Net lists well over 15,000 groups worldwide. This number does not include the many environmental groups and other social movement groups that care about animal issues—these are described in interesting ways by Paul Hawken in his creatively titled 2007 book, *Blessed Unrest: How the Largest Movement in the World Came into Being, and Why No One Saw It Coming.*

Is it now possible to tell the full story of the humans' efforts at animal protection?

The history and diversity of modern animal protection movements, and in particular local protectionists' creative responses to *local* problems relevant to each specific culture, suggest strongly that many humans break through to animal protection even when governments and influential institutions in law, religion, and education play down animal protection. For this reason alone, the continuing story of wide-ranging and local responses to specific problems is a developing, diverse, and complicated story. Because responses are occurring quickly around the world, the story is still to be told in detail.

What has been particularly helpful in recognizing how rich the overall historical and present stories are is the fact that many different people have worked to identify different pieces of the puzzle. This is one reason that the multifaceted or "interdisciplinary" approach is emphasized in this book. As a species, we are increasingly more knowledgeable about all animal categories. This is particularly true of companion animals, but we also have learned a great deal about our possibilities and problems with the animals we put into our category "food animals" as well as the ethical problems and scientific limits of using living beings as "research animals," and we continue to explore and make astonishing discoveries about wildlife.

Today we recognize that human societies are only at midpoint in the story, and there is much future still to be chosen. One important new contributor to our telling of this story is the emerging field of animal studies. As mentioned in chapter 8, this field is really an umbrella under which sit many disciplines, such as history, literature, and many other familiar fields. These disciplines are now found in the subdivision of university education known generally as "the humanities." For reasons suggested in chapter 8, "higher education" is likely to be more effective if the "sciences and humanities" dualism is expanded to a more realistic "science, humanities, and animals studies" approach.

5

LAWS

As one of humans' most significant institutions, legal systems have impacted greatly the ways in which humans deal with other living beings. There are several different kinds of legal systems around the world, and while most of the discussion here focuses on the legal tradition known generally as the common law tradition, the general principles discussed also apply to other major legal traditions such as the civil law traditions, Islamic law, and indigenous legal traditions.

The style of legal system that has come to be known as "common law" originated in England. It is an approach to law making that gives great deference to custom and general principles as they are embodied in cases decided by judges—these cases serve as precedent and are applied to situations not covered by laws that a legislature has passed. Common law systems are found in a wide range of countries, including Australia, Brunei, Canada, Ghana, Hong Kong, India, Ireland, Kenya, Malaysia, New Zealand, Pakistan, Singapore, South Africa, Sri Lanka, Tanzania, and the United States.

The common law tradition has been a pioneer in the use of "rights" as a legal way of thinking. Since legal systems are the place where *legal* rights are worked out, discussions about animal rights, whether of the moral or legal sort, go much better when the status of nonhumans under law is clearly understood. It is also important to recognize that today there is a vibrant field called "animal law," in which the present status and future possibilities of animal protection are being thoroughly discussed.

What is the (traditional) law on animals?

Traditionally, law has treated animals outside our species as mere property of humans. The earliest law codes, such as the Babylonian Code of Hammurabi from about 1750 B.C.E., recognize some domesticated animals as valuable property. The English word "pecuniary" (pertaining to money) derives from the Latin word *pecu* (cattle or flock). Another key word in the common law tradition learned by every first-year law student is "chattel," which is related to the word "cattle" and means an item of personal property that is movable.

Although it was cattle that provided an influential model for development of legal ideas of what could and could not be property (inanimate things also provided a model for the property idea), it was not merely domesticated animals that could be owned. The Code of Justinian, an extremely influential systematization of Roman law from the sixth century C.E., provides explicitly, "Wild beasts, birds, fish and all animals, which live either in the sea, the air, or the earth, so soon as they are taken by anyone, immediately become by the law of nations the property of the captor."

This approach to other living beings impacts us to this day. The American jurist Oliver Wendell Holmes Jr., in his 1881 book *The Common Law*, observed, "So far as concerns the influence of Roman law upon our own,... the evidence of it is to be found in every book which has been written for the last five hundred years." The tradition by which law subordinates all nonhuman animals to human interests impacts not only today's legal systems but also many other areas of society. For example, throughout industrialized societies the subordination of nonhumans to humans has become a principal way of thinking about humans' relationship to the other-than-human world.

Along with various religious ideas about the importance of humans, law has promoted a general tendency to broad generalizations about humans' superior status in the world, such that people today assume that it is "natural" that any and all nonhuman animals are rightly reduced to property owned by individual humans or by the rulers of the state generally. This tendency to subordinate the natural world is not news to anyone today, and the aggressiveness and arrogance of this approach in legal systems are matched by the long history of some powerful humans treating other, less powerful *humans* as personal property that could be owned.

There are many reasons, then, that the majority of people today share the idea that nonhuman animals, whether valued as livestock or as wild resources to be captured, naturally fall into the property category. This is one reason today's legal systems characteristically claim to protect all members of the human species within their jurisdiction (the realities are often not so beautiful), while protections for nonhuman animals, when they exist, are of a different category altogether.

Yet, as noted at any number of points in this book, talk about moral and legal protections for some nonhuman animals is now common. Many readers will know that, historically, some nonhuman animals were offered protections in the part of law known generally as criminal law and more specifically as anticruelty protections. But this kind of protection for the animals themselves is, *within the law*, a relatively new development that began in the nineteenth century. The courts that over centuries developed the common law tradition did not develop any rules regarding prohibition of cruelty to other living beings. This is partly because anticruelty prohibitions already were nurtured by other institutions and value systems, such as religious communities. Further, a basic assumption of the law during the early period of the common law tradition was that other living beings were intended for humans' use. Anticruelty protections were aimed, on the whole, at deviant individuals, not at society-wide practices and values. If a practice was cruel but was widespread within a society, there was no chance that the anticruelty provisions would be invoked.

Another peculiarity can be found in the way in which philosophers who addressed the nature of these cruelty-sensitive rules explained the rules' purpose. Thomas Aquinas and Immanuel Kant, two of the western tradition's most significant philosophers, offered explanations of anticruelty guidelines that focused on the benefits for *humans* that this kind of protection brought. They reasoned that the justification for anticruelty provisions was that an individual human who hurt nonhumans might then go on to hurt the really important beings, namely, humans. Nonetheless, most common people assumed in the past, as they do today, that anticruelty protections were for the sake of the nonhumans, not humans.

The upshot of these legal and philosophical traditions has generally been that society plays down the protections that legal systems offer to nonhumans of any kind. This is one reason that most of the past writing about cruelty to other-than-human animals comes not from people focusing on law but from religious figures. When law-inspired writers do mention other animals, the overwhelming focus is on property issues involving human interests. The interests of the nonhuman animals themselves are almost always invisible.

There are some peculiar traditions in which nonhuman animals were tried before courts—these are wonderfully summarized in a 1906 book by E. P. Evans with the revealing title *The Criminal Prosecution and Capital Punishment of Animals: The Lost History of Europe's Animal Trials.* But as a general matter, the presence of nonhuman animals in law discussions is that of mere property, not sentient subjects capable of relationship or suffering or intelligence.

A number of judges and legal commentators, though, have broken through to the commonsense proposition that nonhuman animals might themselves be worthy of legal protections. In 1888, the Supreme Court of the State of Mississippi suggested as it ruled on an anticruelty statute, "This statute is for the benefit of animals, as creatures capable of feeling and suffering, and it was intended to protect them from cruelty, without reference to their being property, or to the damages which might thereby be occasioned to their owners."

Some of the most famous commentators on law have also observed that anticruelty protections are rightly thought of as for the animals. John Chipman Gray of Harvard wrote in his 1921 *The Nature and Sources of the Law* that "certain acts of cruelty...may be forbidden, at least conceivably, for the sake of the creatures themselves."

But even if some of the best known commentators thought of the suffering of other-than-human animals as morally important, the overwhelming majority of legal commentators by the end of the nineteenth century followed the tradition of discussing animals as *mere* property. This explains why the first comprehensive treatise on law and animals in the common law tradition published in the United States treats other living beings solely as property. John Ingham's 1900 volume *The Law of Animals* included a subtitle that mentions "rights," but this is a clear reference to humans' rights: "A Treatise on Property in Animals Wild and Domestic and the Rights and Responsibilities Arising Therefrom." This treatise contains virtually nothing about the various ways in which legal systems can be used to protect non-human animals as valuable beings *in and of themselves.*

But values changed dramatically in the following century. Exactly 100 years after Ingham published his book, a group of lawyers published the first edition of the casebook *Animal Law.* The editors of this new casebook clearly employed a radically different approach to law. Rather than focusing merely on property law, they considered the wide range of ways in which legal systems' underlying principles and other features, such as enforcement realities, impact the living beings around us. The editors included wide-ranging materials on both legal and moral rights for other animals, as well as information about the link between violence against humans and violence against animals.

No one who encountered this new casebook could doubt that the editors had concerns that were, colloquially speaking, "pro-animal" and on the "animal rights" side of the continuum. While the questions and comments are mostly about companion animals, the editors clearly reflect the diversity of early twenty-first-century discussion about other animals.

What is happening today in "animal law"?

One can best see the profound changes that are taking place in this general area by considering what is happening in four specific categories—legal education, litigation in courts, legislation by government bodies, and enforcement of the existing laws.

Legal Education

"Animal law" has become a distinct field in the last decade, and the history of this development is striking. When Harvard Law School adopted its first animal law course in 2000 as a result of petitions signed by scores of students year after year, the American legal education establishment took notice, even though fewer than a dozen American law schools then offered such a course. By the year 2002, more than 40 of the almost 200 law schools accredited by the American Bar Association offered such a course. As of spring 2010, the number of American law schools offering at least one animal law course will exceed 130. This tenfold increase within a decade has been driven by student requests.

Litigation

In some societies, but in particular in the United States, there has been a venerable tradition of using courts to test approaches to social change since the nineteenth century. Feminists, civil rights activists, and environmentalists have pioneered a variety of approaches. Animal protectionists have tried for decades to use any number of the different aspects of this extremely important law-making feature of courts.

What makes litigation an attractive option are two important features of courts. First, the common law legal systems offer a wide range of citizens access to judges who are powerful decision makers and, at least nominally, are committed to following important principles like justice and equality. Second, it is the legal system that often holds certain oppressions in place, a feature that makes *legal* challenges possible and often reasonable.

The goals of litigation involving animals have been quite diverse, ranging from, on the one hand, simply getting a matter heard by a judge to, on the other hand, attempts to force abolition of widespread practices. In general, the goal of these diverse challenges is to test what is possible through courts for the purpose of creating awareness and eventually stopping the harms that some humans do as a matter of course to nonhuman animals.

There are many hurdles to litigation-based attempts to alter existing laws and traditions that adversely impact nonhuman animals. For example, when it comes to suing on behalf of non-human animals, as a practical matter only lawyers are integrally involved in this kind of litigation because licensing requirements and other technicalities create barriers in courts for nonlawyers. But even though litigation is technically challenging, this is an approach where lawyers speak to lawyers about ideals like justice, equity, dignity, and freedom.

The details of litigation all over the world are too complex to describe in anything shorter than a multivolume encyclopedia. In summary, it can be said that there have already been many challenges on behalf of many different animals. A few judges have ruled that certain animals have "rights," but it remains generally true that rights-based language in courts is only just beginning to be explored (an example is mentioned in chapter 6).

The following story introduces key elements that play out in litigation, and also offers insights into why challenges to the property status of nonhuman animals is a central issue. Since humans are the owners of those animals held to be legal property, challenging the property status of animals means challenging rights held by humans. But the attitudes and realities that drive the following story make it possible to imagine why this is important to so many today. This story comes out of the state of New Jersey in the United States, where there is little legal protection for the vast majority of farm animals. This passage, which is drawn from Scully's *Dominion*, portrays well the dismissive attitude toward other living beings that can prevail in law.

> Just how bereft of human feeling that entire industry has become was clear at a municipal court case heard in Warren County, New Jersey, in the fall of 2000. A poultry company...was convicted of cruelly discarding live chickens in trash cans. The conviction was appealed and overturned, partly on the grounds that [the corporate owner]...had only six employees overseeing 1.2 million laying hens, and with workers each left to tend two hundred thousand creatures it remained unproven they were aware of those particular birds dying in a trash can. The company's initial defense...asserted outright that this is exactly what the birds were anyway—trash:
>
> ATTORNEY TO THE JUDGE: We contend, Your Honor, that clearly my client meets the requirements [of the law]. Clearly it's a commercial farm. And clearly the handling of chickens, and how chickens are discarded, falls into agricultural management practices of my client. And...we've litigated this issue before in this county with respect to my client and how it handles its manure....
>
> JUDGE: Isn't there a big distinction between manure and live animals?

ATTORNEY: No, Your Honor. Because the Right to Farm Act protects us in the operation of our farm and all of the agricultural management practices employed by our firm.

The legal conclusion drawn by this lawyer reveals poignantly how decidedly a modern industrialized society can, through its laws, deny the simplest of realities that all of us know to be true. It also reveals that, under the version of "animal law" that prevails for production animals, the status "legal thing," reducing living beings to mere resources, can be cruel beyond our imagination. Most people would hold that discarding live chickens without moral qualm, or that referring to them as the equivalent of manure, runs *completely* counter to our cultural heritage in favor of compassion for living beings.

What much contemporary litigation regarding animals represents, as do demands for animal law courses and political attempts to change practices through letter writing and any number of other techniques, is a challenge to those who ignore the most basic anticruelty considerations. Simply said, production processes that treat other living beings as mere property are controversial enough to engender both concern and social activism. Lawyers' use of litigation to challenge such harms thus reflects core *moral* values sitting at the heart of animal rights concerns.

Litigation is more than just reaction to radical subordination of other animals. Many filed lawsuits attempt preemptive changes and even abolition. But by and large the general phenomenon of using courts is meant to shine light on problems. The hope is to use the existing power of courts to, in one way or another, reinstate our human cultures' long-standing commitment to the central importance of compassion and anticruelty values.

Litigation-based approaches to problems have their limits for a variety of reasons. Judges often respond that if they intervene in a problem, they will usurp the law-making role of elected legislatures. But litigation, which has had a high profile in the first 30 years of the animal law movement, will likely continue to be used regularly in those legal systems which permit this form of challenge.

Legislation

Around the world today, legislation is the primary vehicle of animal law, even in the United States legal system, where court-based challenges have been extremely important in animal protection and many other social movements. In general, legislation in nation after nation reflects the ferment described in this book.

Sometimes, proposed legislation builds on existing protections, as in India where the nation's founding document itself (which became effective in 1948) calls out the importance of animal protection. In a section titled "Fundamental Duties," the Constitution of India states plainly, "It shall be the duty of every citizen of India...to have compassion for living creatures." Animal laws in India are common, as can be seen in the sheer size of the volume *Animal Laws of India* edited by two leaders of the Indian animal protection movement described in chapter 10.

Constitution-level provisions are important because constitutions are a kind of super-legislation providing the foundation on which all subsequent legislation and litigation are based. Amending a constitution to include other-than-human animals is, then, a very significant act. In the summer of 2002, Germany became the first country in the European Union to guarantee constitution-level protection to any nonhuman animals when that nation's constitution was amended to include the words "and the animals" in Section 20A, which now provides: "[t]he State, in a spirit of responsibility for future generations, also protects the natural living conditions and the animals within the framework of the constitutional rules through the legislation and as provided by the laws through the executive power and the administration of justice."

Because not all nation states have constitutions, and because it is still rare in industrialized nations that animal protection is a topic explicitly dealt with at this high level, specific legislation has long played the central role in what a society will do via its legal system for other-than-human animals. Today, thousands of legislative proposals are made, and hundreds pass each year.

It is also significant that legislation can be enacted in ways that do not involve a vote by the elected legislative body. This has been particularly significant in the United States, where voters are often permitted within specific states to vote directly on "ballot measures" or "popular initiatives." Between 1940 and 1990, there were only a half dozen such initiatives on animal issues. But since 1990, there have been in the range of 50 animal-related initiatives of this kind. Many involved hunting issues, but the high-profile success of three farm animal initiatives passed through the efforts of animal protection organizations in the last decade suggests that the food animal issue is now on the political map in the United States. The most significant of these initiatives was in California, the most populous American state. In 2008, by a large majority (63+%) California voters passed an initiative banning certain housing practices for egg-laying chickens, veal calves, and pregnant sows.

An interesting example of how the term "rights" is used even in legal circles was published a year after this election. The November 2009 edition of the *California Bar Journal*, the official publication of the state's lawyer association, included a front-page story in which the chief justice of the California Supreme Court attempted to deride the election results by alluding to another ballot vote that prohibited same-sex marriages: "Chickens gained valuable rights in California on the same day that gay men and lesbians lost them." Importantly, the successful animal protection legislation involved *no specific legal rights* for the farm animals which are its subjects. This judge's comment reflects how common it is to speak generically of "rights," even when the legal protections put into place fall far short of specific legal rights. This is the traditional sense of the word "rights" invoked by many people when they refer to "animal rights."

Another legislation-based approach involves a government agency issuing detailed administrative regulations that control humans' interactions with other living beings. These are commonly used in hunting, handling, or importation of wildlife, development of land that impacts environmental issues, and research using animals.

Yet another legislative approach is to create administrative advocacy for nonhuman animals. A creative use of such an arrangement appears in Switzerland's Canton of Zurich, where the local government employs a lawyer to take the role of advocating on behalf of nonhuman animals themselves.

The enactment of laws or regulations is only a first step in a very complex process. For a variety of reasons, in many countries there are laws "on the books," as the saying goes, which are not enforced. For this reason, the next section deals with the realities of enforcement, for these speak unerringly about what a society's real public policy is.

Enforcement

Laws "on the books" may seem impressive, but they can be made ineffective by dishonest or questionable interpretations, and also by simple lack of enforcement. So a critical issue in animal rights discussions is administration or enforcement of laws.

Lack of enforcement takes many different forms. For example, as a practical matter, when prosecutors are asked to prosecute juveniles who have treated shelter animals cruelly, or even killed them, such prosecutors often have chosen not to try the juveniles because there is no political will to spend taxpayer dollars for this priority. Another form of lack of enforcement is the subterfuge mentioned in chapter 2 by which regulators in the United States charged with enforcing a federal law governing research animal protections chose arbitrarily to exclude rats, mice, and birds. Lack of enforcement can also become a reality for fiscal reasons—there exist in a number of countries today, for example, any number of animal protection mandates, like humane education requirements, that are unfunded and thus unrealized.

The fact that laws "on the books" are not enforced is important because those seeking effective enforcement of existing laws have at times been labeled "animal rights advocates," even though they seek no change in the formal law but only action on laws already approved.

What is the role of legal rights in "animal rights" debates?

Legal rights can play a distinctive role in animal protection for a number of reasons. First, legal rights are characteristically *specific*, because a legislature or judge in a court has had to create them. When they are created, legal rights are given some sort of definition or description so that those who must enforce them have an idea of what the lawmakers intended when creating the legal right at issue. This also means that legal rights are usually defined in a specific place that ordinary citizens can access when trying to figure out what and who existing laws protect.

Second, legal rights are usually held by someone or something. It is common to think of legal rights as held by individuals, but corporations and other collections of individuals can be the holder of legal rights.

Third, legal rights are widely believed to be the highest form of legal protection. This is not always true in actual practice for two reasons. Legal rights are not as absolute as some claim—they can be, and sometimes are, overridden by the government. (We all agree, for example, that it is acceptable to curtail the free speech rights of those tempted to yell "Fire!" in a crowded theater.) In addition, other legal protections can in some instances be even more effective than individual rights—if a society outlaws ownership of, say, chimpanzees, this legal tool can be far more effective at curtailing problems than giving a captive chimpanzee a right to be free from cruelty.

It is the psychological and political value of granting an individual "rights" that makes legal rights for animals so valuable. When a group of beings is so recognized, they have arrived in terms of not only legal protections but also political, social, and ethical protections. In this sense, legal rights are extremely important because they reinforce moral versions of animal rights.

The attempt to use the legal rights tool for the purpose of protecting some favored beings *outside the human species* is, in one sense, natural enough, given that this tool is so important in modern political systems. But a full assessment of the role of specific legal rights for nonhuman animals must be supplemented with a realistic appraisal of some practical problems.

First, despite the importance of legal rights, talk about these high level protections is, as suggested in chapter 3, undisciplined and vague. This is why, among legal scholars, there is no consensus on what rights mean for humans. Further, on the question of whether *existing* legal protections for animals already in place grant "legal rights" to animals, there is no agreement (this is discussed further in chapter 6).

Second, as the discussion above on enforcement problems makes clear, the political will does not always exist to enforce specific protections, including "rights," that are "on the books." Third, the granting of legal rights and other forms of legal protection to a new group usually involves some loss of power and privilege for someone. In the same way that giving women legal rights curtailed men's legal rights to dominate women, giving legal protections to some nonhuman animals will curtail at least some human privileges now in place. Examples are given in chapter 6 about the risk of job losses, for some change is unavoidable.

Importantly, though, even if it is not always clear what problems the granting of legal rights will involve, this remains an altogether powerful and popular tool. For those cases where there is a treasured class of animals that many in human society insist receive the maximum protection available under law, there will be attempt after attempt to get lawmakers to grant specific legal rights to these treasured beings.

What is the significance of the "rights versus welfare" debate?

One of the principal ways of talking about animal protection contrasts an "animal rights" approach with an approach called "animal welfare." This common "rights *versus* welfare" dualism has limited value because the contrast can be misleading for a variety of reasons.

One reason the dualism misleads is that, as we have seen, "animal rights" has meant a variety of things. The term still is used widely in its original sense of moral protections for certain animals, including compassion and respect for life. Concern for "welfare" or the well-being of individuals is an integral part of this original, morals-driven approach to animal *rights*. The dualism "rights *versus* welfare" promotes only a minor sense of animal welfare, even as it ignores the far more substantial idea of welfare that has long been a key element in morals-based protections for nonhuman animals. The more substantial idea of welfare involves the animals' freedom from harms like captivity and pain, as well as the freedom to move around. When any of these important freedoms is violated, as it so often is when the minor sense of "animal welfare" prevails, there is very little true "welfare" that is being proposed. Thus, drawing a sharp contrast along the lines of "rights *versus* welfare" contradicts the original meaning of "animal rights," which in *every* respect holds concern for the welfare of individual animals to be of the utmost importance.

A second way in which the "rights *versus* welfare" dualism tends to mislead is related—many people today use the idea of "animal welfare" to preserve human domination over certain animals. Some advocates of human superiority have rationalized humans' domination over other living beings by focusing on attempts to ameliorate in minor ways the terrible conditions that such domination creates for animals. Such rationalizations lead some to think that when we concede minor welfare improvements to farm animals or research animals, our domination of these animals is "gentler" or "less harsh," and thus ethically adequate. This version of "animal welfare" leads with the suggestion "let's improve their welfare" *but at the same time* maintains the right of humans to total domination as we do experiments on them or use them for food or resources.

Upon examination, then, many calls for "animal welfare reform" are fundamentally inconsistent with the original sense of "animal welfare" that takes seriously the claim that animals matter in and of themselves. Welfare provisions used to soften humans' sense of guilt are, at best, watered-down versions of the original insight that respecting an animal's welfare is an important goal. Many contemporary calls for "welfare improvements" fall far short of the husbandry contract described in chapter 2; they also are far less significant than the rules that were developed for religious slaughter briefly described in chapter 6.

When "animal welfare" comes to mean primarily that tough conditions for the animal are made better in some minor respect, with no mention at all of the original, major sense of "animal welfare," the meaning of the word "welfare" has been stretched so dramatically that it misleads. Everyone thus needs to know that "animal welfare" is sometimes used in this strained way by those who are overwhelmingly driven by *human* interests. When narrow and clearly minor changes in practice that amount to very little change in the life of the animals involved are called "welfare improvements," such a claim obscures and confuses, thus harming listeners' ability to make informed moral choices.

Despite such tensions in its use, the habit of referring to "animal welfare" remains widespread. Two reasons for the term's popularity are political in nature. First, surely the animals subjected to unrelenting harms and an inevitable death would vote to have their situation ameliorated even in minor ways. This fact leads some people to support even minor welfare reforms. But when talk of "animal welfare" remains exclusively focused on talk of bigger cages, of animals in confinement being allowed to turn around or merely stretch their limbs, the result may be political advantage for those who use animals, because the claim that "animal welfare" is being advanced through such minor concessions is used to blunt criticism of the overall harshness, even cruelty, of the profound domination still exercised over captive animals.

Clarity about "animal welfare" and "improvements" requires that we factor in what conditions and harms still prevail *after* the "welfare improvements" are in place. The absence of frank discussion of such realities is one reason some critics have repudiated what they call the "welfarist" position. These critics see minor concessions as political cover for continued human domination that on a daily basis harms the animals so terribly that "welfare" is not a term that would normally come to mind.

A second sense in which strategies focusing on "animal welfare" are political in nature is more positive. Contemporary political realities (described in chapter 7) have often been so unfavorable to nonhuman animals that, in the short term, only minor welfare reforms, not abolition-like reforms, are possible. This has meant that activists dedicated to eliminating harms have recognized that they can only get to their goal one step at a time. Some activists have thus reasoned that they *must* get as much done now as possible, which as a political reality means accepting welfare "improvements" of the kind that the captive animals themselves would likely favor. Such activists may in no way acquiesce in the right of humans to total domination of the animals whose welfare is slightly improved; instead, such activists often vow to continue work toward a next step that amounts to change of a kind that would fit truer senses of "animal welfare."

There is a substantial debate in the animal rights community over whether incremental change strategies are effective. Historical examples from the antislavery, women's suffrage, and civil rights movements suggest strongly that incremental changes can, over time, play a critical role in creating fundamental social change. But this road is by no means an easy one, for those who wish to create fundamental change take a number of risks by seeking only partial, incremental changes. The greatest of these risks is the possibility that incremental changes will lock harmful practices permanently into place. Much more work needs to be done to assess whether those confined by political realities to achieving only minor "welfare improvements" help or hurt oppressed groups. It remains the conclusion of many animal rights advocates that even if the implementation of welfare changes leaves animals in very harsh circumstances, this strategy creates political awareness that can be mobilized in the future for far more effective protections and even abolition of the harms that are being done. Some even suggest that this "welfare first" approach can lead ultimately to protections that are in the nature of true legal rights.

Thus, although the "rights *versus* welfare" debate can mislead if it is not nuanced, true concerns for animal welfare remain part of the political landscape of today's animal rights movement, even though they are complicated and potentially risky. The diminishment of harm, which incremental changes seek, is one of the most important of all ethical principles, and some version of it is found in every ethical system humans have created. But when achieving a reduction in harm is minor and does not relieve the source of oppression, there is obviously reason for continuing concern. The risk will always remain that a compromise leaving fundamental harms in place not only affirms the morality of the underlying practice but *strengthens* the right to harm. This is a serious risk in industrialized societies where calls for "welfare" have characteristically been about animals used as mere resources.

The dualism "rights *versus* welfare" tends to prevail in countries where private property rights are politically so popular that people and businesses can cite them as controlling and thereby obscure the moral issues arising out of domination of other living beings. Such a strategy keeps existing privileges over other animals intact because it relies on a very distorted and impoverished notion of "welfare." Elsewhere, "animal welfare" is a more robust concept along the lines of true moral protections for other animals because the latter matter in and of themselves.

What is possible under today's developing animal law?

Even among traditional commentators who assert that there is nothing at all wrong with *human-centered* law, one finds recognition that legal systems can protect other living beings. This recognition goes beyond anticruelty protections discussed in this chapter. Gray observed in his 1921 volume, "It is quite conceivable, however, that there may have been, or indeed, may still be, systems of Law in which animals have legal rights, for instance, cats in ancient Egypt, or white elephants in Siam."

Because human societies long ago reached the conclusion that our relationships with other living beings raise inevitable ethical issues, it is understandable that people today call upon our legal systems' different tools, including specific legal rights, to shield those nonhuman individuals that we elect to protect. Further, if we deem it the ethical thing to do, we can put in place very high-level protections for some nonhuman animals, such as granting them the status of "legal persons." There is no logical contradiction in using the law in this way, for even though the elegant scholar Gray viewed such an option as not right for his time, he honestly observed in his 1921 treatise, "animals may conceivably be legal persons."

The ongoing maturation of animal law and the emergence of animal studies (discussed in chapter 8) help everyone to recognize that we have inherited a wide range of possibilities from the many cultures that have for thousands of years considered the importance of animal protection. Because we can now be candid that our own species' record on treating other living beings, including humans, is mixed, we are in the position to go forward with law, education, science, and ethics in creative ways. We can call out how strained many claims are in the present polarized environment where nonhuman animals' status is discussed. Those who repudiate animal rights in any form because they assert that humans alone deserve moral protections miss the benefits which animal protection has often brought to the human community.

One goal of the modern animal studies field discussed in chapter 8 is use of critical thinking skills not only in the field but in education broadly. John Harris in his essay included in the 1971 book *Animals, Man and Morals: An Enquiry into the Maltreatment of Non-Humans* challenged those who consider traditional and contemporary reasoning about the human/ nonhuman divide to avoid mere rationalization to justify existing practices, greed, blind habit, and self-aggrandizement. Nonetheless, it is hard to deny that such rationalizations remain a principal element of the polarized debate over both moral and legal versions of animal rights.

The fact that humans have created flexible legal systems suitable to protecting not only humans but nonhumans as well suggests that the future is likely to be one in which there are many calls to use an array of the available tools to craft meaningful animal protection of many different kinds. Societies are already using legislative means in a variety of ways, such as outlawing ownership of specific animals as a way to preclude insensitive humans from doing harm to those animals. Other legal tools can also be used to create *fundamental, effective legal protections.* Even the concept of property ownership can be shaped in ways that create *fundamental legal protections* for the owned beings—owners can be given duties of care that match or even outweigh their privileges. There is nothing whatsoever absolute in the notion of property rights that requires that owners have complete power over their property. Every society now regulates property use in a variety of ways, such as zoning rules governing how owners use land. Anticruelty laws operate as limitations on dog or cat owners (one cannot, for example, beat one's dog with a baseball bat).

The key is that legal tools are flexible, and with the appropriate grassroots support reasonable policies for ownership responsibilities can be developed. This flexibility sets the stage for an intriguing question for our entire society today—what will the *future* of laws regarding nonhuman animals be?

Two facts will impact greatly what happens. One is already in place—dramatic change has taken place within the last century and begun to open minds to the multiple meanings of animal rights. The second fact deals with the pace of change— that pace is now, if anything, increasing, but where the changes will lead us is up to us as individuals, for *we* guide our governments, corporations, cultures, and thus our species as a whole. So the obvious question is, what shape will we give laws affecting nonhuman animals in the coming years?

The general possibilities are not yet known, although these are considered in the final section of this book. Such considerations beg the question of whether law is the *leading* element in attitudes toward animals, or in fact is a secondary element that takes its cue from changes in social attitudes regarding certain categories of animals, such as companion animals.

Is it likely that law, lawyers, and legislation will lead our societies in changes regarding the status of animals?

In the different legal systems around the world, there are respected traditions of legal philosophers, judges, and lawyers leading important discussions on social values and proposed changes in society. Since animal law is without question one of the leading areas of both the animal protection movement and the burgeoning educational movement known as animal studies, it is important to focus on what roles law and societies' judges and lawyers might play regarding the status of other-than-human animals.

Throughout this book, there are references to the fact that many other segments of human society—businesses, nonprofit groups, the veterinary profession, religious communities, educational institutions, veterinarians, scientific studies—will have input that will make future legal changes possible or impossible. One answer to the question of whether lawyers will lead all of us is that judges, lawyers, and legal philosophers will surely be in the front ranks of the movement going forward. It is not likely, however, that this group will have all of the insights needed to direct other groups as our society deals with the living beings outside our species.

As to who might also be in the front ranks as our societies go forward on animal protection, one group of contributors is likely to be critical thinkers, including philosophers, policy analysts, and those who study multiple cultures, for these individuals will have insights into what options are now being used around the world. In addition, those who study the wide variety of ways other-than-human animals are being engaged in sciences, the arts, and our humanities fields will be needed.

There are features of the newly emerged field of animal law that suggest that law is but one contributor among others as we go forward. Animal law is gaining prominence in legal education and in lawyer organizations, and this trend constitutes what might be thought of as the first wave of animal law. The second wave is only now reaching the shore as graduates of the hundreds of animal law courses take their place in the ranks of lawyers, organization leaders, government regulators, and business leaders. The second wave of animal law will be more interdisciplinary, for insights into the future must come from the broader society as we engage the human/animal intersection in countless different ways. Answers to questions about which beings deserve justice come not only from law and lawyers but equally from ethics, religion, conscience, social debate, and much more. The end product of this debate is then, hopefully, reflected in the laws enacted.

Already, individual lawyers and philosophers of law—a good example is Steven M. Wise, described in chapter 10—have shown how flexible and capable the legal system can be *if* one uses basics commitments already in place in legal systems to justice, fairness, ethics, and scientific expertise. Given our capacious human imagination, those who go forward from this point into second- and third-wave animal law will stand on the shoulders of such people but will no doubt see much further and better as our societies talk together over the next decades about what we would like to do with humans' abilities to care about animals of all kinds.

This brief discussion of which areas of our rich human societies must be involved in animal rights opens up the questions of the following sections regarding political and social realities today.

6

POLITICAL REALITIES

Long-standing problems of humans harming other humans still command enormous amounts of time in our political discussions, even as new issues like global warming and public health threats clamor for attention. Whether morally based concerns for harms to other animals will be given a voice in future political discussions is a hotly debated topic. Politics, it turns out, has long been extremely narrow-minded. The words "political," "policy," "police," and "polite" stem from the Greek word *polis*, which means "city." Since Greek cities were typically walled off from the outside world, discussions of city-based matters and passions were understandably not particularly connected to nonhuman animals. While there were some ancient discussions driven by passions for "countryside" or "nature," and today in some political discussions people talk of "the environment" and even "wilderness," the concerns that most decisively *shape* political discussions still remain human-centered in ways that cause participants *not* to consider the relevance of animals to much of human life.

What are the political realities for animals today?

The discussions regarding animal issues now going forward in individual societies and their legislatures, as well as in the global community generally, are pushed by a diverse range of citizens from different sectors of society. Creative approaches in one country have opened up new possibilities in other societies, just as successes in one country have given citizens of other countries hope that they can pass comparable protections at home. Ferment around the world is, thus, a factor in many local political systems.

Another important factor that impacts greatly what is possible in the political realm is the existence of cultural traditions already mentioned in chapter 4. One area of cultural practices that decisively affects political possibilities is the psychologically and economically important area of eating practices. Horsemeat consumption remains prevalent in France and other countries despite revulsion at this traditional practice in many societies. Dogs are eaten in parts of East Asia, much to the consternation of people from cultures where dogs are now widely held to be family members. The same people who revere dogs often consume beef without a second thought, a fact which causes those who hold cattle sacred, as is the case in India, to react with moral condemnation.

Differences in political traditions also impact greatly what changes are possible in any society. In England and some of the northern European nations, much can be done on animal issues at the national level by way of government action, due to long traditions of the whole society being concerned with the protection of animals. In other countries, like the United States, the prevalence of rhetoric about private property rights, the dominance of economics-based calculations, and the political clout of the huge corporations that control slaughter and meat packing have made political developments at the national level far harder.

Some governments have entire departments focused on animal advocacy, whereas other governments are dominated by agencies driven by resource utilization. Some government agencies are driven by a mentality that favors hunting and control when animals are considered valuable and extermination when they are considered "pests" (as often has happened with wolves).

So cultural and political heritage are obvious factors that open up, or limit, how citizens in different countries experience political possibilities, interpret what is moral or not, and are able to act via governmental mechanisms at the national or more local levels. Further, even when *national* political realities remain decisively human-centered, this has not meant that *local* political possibilities for protecting nonhuman animals are nonexistent.

What successes have there been in politics?

Different kinds of successes have come at different periods of the modern era. In the first half of the nineteenth century, important new laws were passed in England. This started the trend of using government-based action for animal protection. Private organizations and quasi-governmental organizations (such as Britain's Royal Society for the Prevention of Cruelty to Animals) also addressed societal problems.

In the tumultuous twentieth century dominated by two world wars, the second half of the century saw important animal protection legislation enacted in both the United States and Europe. In 1966, the American Congress passed legislation (later known as the Animal Welfare Act) that contained provisions for protecting *all* warm-blooded animals used in laboratories. But as mentioned in chapters 2 and 5, administrative regulations were used arbitrarily to limit the impact of the law on the animals most frequently used in research. Environmental laws were also enacted across borders, such as the 1916 convention between the United States and Great Britain (for Canada), which protected migratory birds, and the 1992 Convention on Biological Diversity, while in individual countries important laws were passed that gave wildlife important new protections for nonhuman animals—in the United States, for example, among the most important legislation were the Marine Mammal Protection Act and the Endangered Species Act.

In Europe, some of the most far-reaching animal protection successes were enacted in the late twentieth century and early twenty-first century. Britain, for example, passed its most comprehensive animal protection legislation in 2006. Through "conventions" or general laws enacted by the Council of Europe, detailed rules now impact farm animal welfare before and during slaughter, transport of animals, the use of animals in research, wildlife and its habitat, and a wide variety of companion animal issues. The latter protections, which shield companion animals from even those formerly common veterinary practices such as ear cropping and tail docking, push developments in other countries where such protections are not possible at the national level and only now are being proposed at the local level.

Throughout the rest of the world, there have also been many examples reflecting different kinds of political successes at securing government-based protections for certain animals. The following seven examples, which are but the tip of a formidable iceberg, have been chosen because they represent diverse techniques of protection.

Between 1986 and 2009, 43 of the 50 U.S. states amended their criminal laws to make certain acts of cruelty to nonhuman animals a felony. (Such a change means punishments of higher fines and prison terms over one year can be imposed.) Three states already had felony-level penalties available prior to 1986, but they were enacted in 1804, 1887, and 1896. Four states still do not have felony-level penalties available for cruelty violations.

In 1999, the government of New Zealand passed a new Animal Welfare Act that for all practical purposes prohibited experiments on "non-human hominids."

In 2000, the High Court of the State of Kerala, India, handed down a decision explicitly using "rights" language as it addressed circus animals "housed in cramped cages, subjected to fear, hunger, pain, not to mention the undignified way of life they have to live." The court ruled that circus animals are "beings entitled to dignified existence" under the Indian Constitution's Article 21, which protects the right to life with dignity. The court reasoned, "If humans are entitled to fundamental rights, why not animals?" The court went beyond the requirements imposed on citizens by the Constitution of India when it commented, "It is not only our fundamental duty to show compassion to our animal friends, but also to recognise and protect their rights." Other courts in India and one court in Sri Lanka have also used the notion of legal rights for animals.

In 2005, the Austrian parliament agreed to ban experiments on nonhuman apes that are not in the interest of the individual animal. This development was prompted by one of the individuals discussed in chapter 10.

In 2008, the popular referendum in California described in chapter 5 changed how certain farm animals (veal calves, pregnant pigs, and egg-laying chickens) can be housed.

In 2008, Spain's parliament passed a resolution granting legal rights to nonhuman great apes that tracks the fundamental protections long advocated by a nonprofit group known as the Great Ape Project.

In 2009, the Senate of Bolivia approved a law prohibiting the use of wild and domestic animals in circuses.

In summary, there have been, and will be, many different kinds of political successes. We turn next to the other side of the ledger, namely, political failures.

What failures have there been?

The existence of so many successes must be put into the wider context, for legislation in any topic area, including animal protection, is a very complex process. Without question, many legislative efforts have fallen far short of their goals. If hundreds of pieces of animal protection legislation have been passed in the last decade, thousands have been introduced.

The ratio of success to failures is not always revealing, for there is always a certain asymmetry in legislative matters. When a proposal fails, it may be (and very often is) reintroduced the next year. So the ratio of "successes" to "failures" in legislative matters does not alone reveal whether a cause is gaining or losing ground. What matters is the ultimate success of getting the law "on the books." It may or may not be enforced, as discussed in chapter 5, but enactment is important for obvious reasons—it makes the law part of the official record and public policy, and it creates a strong likelihood of enforcement.

Beyond the inevitable failures of proposed legislation being turned down, there are other, more signal kinds of defeats, such as the exclusion of most research animals from the Animal Welfare Act in the United States. Another development that must be marked as a signal failure for animal protection advocates involves farm animals in the United States. This change contrasts markedly with the 1986–2009 successes described above by which felony-level penalties were made available for anticruelty violations. A parallel development from 1985 on has been the *exemption* of farm animals from the anticruelty laws that were originally enacted in the nineteenth century. For example, between 1985–1995, at least 18 of the 50 states in the United States passed laws exempting agribusiness from existing anticruelty laws. Because a dozen states already exempted "accepted," "common," "customary," or "normal" farming practices from anticruelty laws, the result is that a majority of American states now have in place this major alteration in the scope of anticruelty protections. There are two ironies in this development—first, the original laws passed in the early nineteenth century protecting animals were directed at farm animals, and, second, exempting farm animals from anticruelty laws means that most of the animals impacted by consumer choices in the United States are not covered by anti-cruelty protections.

Other important failures of legislation include the 2004 failure in China of the first-ever draft law on protecting animal welfare. Opponents of this new form of Chinese legislation argued that it was impractical and premature in a still-developing nation. The law would have required that all animals be treated in a humane manner, and that farm animals be slaughtered with as little pain as possible. In late 2009, public reactions to dog slaughters and other problems, as well as relatively favorable coverage by state-run media of companion animal rescues, produced renewed discussions about the possibility of anticruelty legislation. Both public reaction and the tone of stories in the state-controlled media suggest that within the last decade the cause of companion animal protection has made significant inroads into Chinese society and may eventually embody some features of the ancient Chinese moral tradition of compassion for other-than-human beings. China has endangered-species legislation but no legislation along the lines of a general animal welfare law. There are international agreements, such as that which governs the World Trade Organization, by which animal protections can still impact China's exports of animal products, but the domestic treatment of nonhuman animals in this most populous nation is by and large still not covered. Since, as noted above, discussion of animal protection is an ongoing process, China will no doubt see another animal welfare law proposed in the future.

Legislation in the area of animal rights is, like legislation in any other area, a constantly shifting balance of "successes and failures." As animal protection concerns spread, mature, and turn to new topics, this balance of failures and successes will be in constant evolution. Some political developments, such as the exemption of farm animals from anticruelty laws or the exclusion of rats and mice from laboratory protections, clearly repudiate the values that drive the animal protection movement. But other political developments just as clearly reveal that the public has deep interest in "animal rights" in the generic sense of law-based and morality-based protections.

While in summary one can only conclude that the story on animal-related legislation is mixed, the accumulation of legislative successes can have much impact beyond the legislative realm. Court-based challenges, which are in part addressed in chapter 5, also involve more failures than successes. But just as is the case with legislation, the fact that a majority of cases do not end up favorably for nonhuman animals may not reflect an overall trend, especially in light of the fact that courts often choose to defer to the democratic process of the legislature. One victory in either legislation or litigation can shift the entire balance in an area of debate.

The following high-profile failure in a court-based case reveals an additional factor involved when animal protectionists use animal rights notions to push for fundamental change. In 2008, an Austrian court refused to grant an animal protection group's petition to have a chimpanzee (whose name was Matthew Hiasl Pan) declared a person so that the court could then name the group as the chimpanzee's legal guardian. The shelter where this individual chimpanzee lived for more than a quarter of a century was bankrupt, threatening to leave Matthew homeless. While donors had offered to help support him, under Austrian law only a legal person can receive personal gifts, and Matthew did not qualify because he was not a member of the human species. This prompted the Vienna-based Association Against Animal Factories to petition the court to be appointed as Matthew's trustee.

That a group could seek to have a chimpanzee legally held to be a person for such purposes was possible in the first decade of the twenty-first century because there have been so many diverse developments around the world regarding the way that societies, through law or otherwise, can protect living beings outside the human species. This case sought to create a precedent in Austria, but it was possible only because so much work by so many other people has opened up legal discussions to these kinds of possibilities.

The Austrian court's denial of legal personhood for Matthew Hiasl Pan was a failure by one measure, but the very raising of the issue creates the possibility that another court at another time may hold differently. Further, the worldwide reporting of this series of events also increased awareness of the possibility of using courts to advance animal protection causes. An alternative is, to be sure, legislation to accomplish precisely the same end.

Attempts to change the law in courts or legislatures can then, even when they are "failures" in the short run, produce important long-term effects that manifest in future discussions around the world. In this sense, creative litigation and legislation are but one step on a long journey whose endpoint is not yet clear. The Austrian case has, for example, been appealed to the European Court of Human Rights.

Assessing "success" or "failure," thus, is a complicated endeavor. The successes that have occurred do not speak to many of the thousands of different problems that arise when humans interact with other living beings. Setbacks and failures can reflect social values other than animal protection, such that even apparent failures can prompt people to find other ways to protect animals. The headings "animal rights" and "animal protection" are so broad that they will surely include many future successes and failures as our species goes forward with questions about living together in a world that necessarily includes many other kinds of living beings.

What is the overall state of today's animal protection movement?

The contemporary animal protection movement, with segments that address a range of specific problems in more than 100 countries, is extraordinarily diverse. Since harms to other living beings are driven by factors as diverse as ignorance, apathy, corporate greed, political corruption, national tradition, and religious conviction, the local and regional movements that seek to counteract and even abolish the many harms done to nonhuman animals are quite naturally diverse as well. Given the pattern of some successes and some failures, one thing is clear—animal protection issues are decidedly in *ferment*.

The fact that animal protection has become a well-known social movement is itself a noteworthy change, for a century ago there was no movement at all outside of anticruelty developments. But with this change have come complications. Resorting to violence to prompt change is a tactic borrowed from other social movements. But the use of violence on behalf of a cause that itself is a protest against violence to animals creates serious problems—it uses as a tool the very thing being protested. Thus those who would use violence on behalf of the animal cause risk a moral contradiction. The animal protection movement proposes a revolution against violence. This revolution is loosely coordinated, multiform, flexible, and based on a common goal rather than on a common blueprint. The goal is, in its most general terms, finding a way for humans and nonhumans to live together whenever possible.

One clear political and social reality is that those who use violence on behalf of an animal cause harm to the overall animal rights movement. The use of violence, however infrequent it may be, has given those who oppose animal protection the chance to paint the entire social movement as a problem. As other portions of this book attest, there are tools that have proven over time to be far more powerful than violence, such as democratic, grassroots work and even civil disobedience in the nonviolent tradition of Gandhi and Thoreau. These are, like court challenges and legislative change, readily available to animal protectionists of all kinds who seek changes in the way any society or business treats other living beings.

The availability of such diverse tools reflects greater public interest and activity today than ever before. This in turn means that today formidable forces clash—there are many grassroots movements for change, but there are some against it as well, just as there are communities of faith on both sides of the debate. Businesses and the educational establishment are entering the fray—in some countries, such as the United States, both business and educational institutions have in the past been decidedly in favor of an exclusively human-centered agenda, but today some businesses and many educational communities take up animal protection causes in important ways.

Overall, then, it must be said that today's animal protection movement is multifaceted, drawing upon communal participation, democratic processes, legal debates, religious and business communities, and a variety of sciences.

What are the prospects in today's societies for legal rights for animals?

Recall the *specific* question that must be asked of the *legal* rights form of animal rights: *which rights for which animals?* With this question in mind, it should be recognized that some respected scholars today assert that some animals already have specific legal protections that are, in fact, legal rights. An example of a highly respected scholar who draws this conclusion is Cass Sunstein, whose views are set out in a 2002 article about animal protections titled "Enforcing Legal Rights." Similarly, Jerrold Tannenbaum, a lawyer and respected veterinary ethicist, has argued that anticruelty provisions in state laws "create legal duties to non-human animals. They therefore afford legal rights to non-human animals."

Other legal scholars disagree, however, because they see legal rights as protections that must not be compromised. Since the legal protections that now are supposed to protect non-human animals are so often compromised or ignored altogether, these dissenting legal scholars conclude that nonhuman animals do not have true legal rights.

Regarding whether any legal system will protect individual nonhumans with specific, legal, and rights-based protections that everyone agrees would be "true animal rights," several things are obvious. First, it is clearly possible that our human community will decide to make such protections part of our laws. Second, there is a serious debate now going forward regarding whether we should do this, and if so, how we might accomplish this step. Third, many people oppose such a move, wanting to reserve "legal rights" for humans alone as a way to signal that humans are more special than other animals.

Equally, though, polls show that many people already approve of some legal rights for some animals *and* that an increasing number of people are open to this possibility.

Importantly, as already noted above, judges in various courts around the world have intentionally used the term "legal rights" for the legal protections that various counties have made available to some animals in some situations. Whether this approach of identifying and enforcing specific legal rights for specific animals (other than humans) will become extremely common or be more occasional, as it is now, remains to be seen.

The beneficiaries of this approach to animal protection are likely to be those animals that are known to be very complex, distinct individuals. Examples include chimpanzees, orangutans, gorillas, bonobos, African and Indian elephants, bottlenose dolphins, orcas, and other cetaceans. Other candidates are certainly companion animals, for many people today think of their dogs as having distinct personalities. The same can be said of cats, horses, and perhaps even the African gray parrot described in Irene Pepperberg's remarkable 2008 book, *Alex & Me: How a Scientist and a Parrot Discovered a Hidden World of Animal Intelligence—and Formed a Deep Bond in the Process.*

Many other animals may well get special legal protections that fall short of true legal rights. Such protections that curtail humans' right to harm other animals can work out to be substantial, even fundamental legal protections, and thus will likely be deemed by many people to be "animal rights" in a generic sense. Still other animals are likely to get legal protections of an incremental sort, such as those that protect minor "welfare" interests as discussed in chapter 5.

As the idea of using fundamental legal protections, even specific legal rights, for other animals becomes more common, it is likely that future generations will resort to this flexible tool more and more often. It is already clear that affording specific legal protections, including legal rights, to specific animals or groups of animals is one way to enact a society's commitment to animal protection.

Legal protections are but one of the ways a society can provide effective safeguards for animals—we turn in the next section to prospects for other forms of "animal rights" in the generic sense of effective, fundamental protections grounded in ethics, morals, religious beliefs, and other human endeavors.

What are the prospects for moral rights?

Moral rights have long been the principal form of animal rights. This form of protection will certainly continue, for legal systems cannot cover all of the important forms of animal protection of which humans are capable. Hence, the moral dimensions that are so evident in daily life among friends, in educational and religious practices and teachings, and in consumer choices and treatment of the natural environment will undoubtedly play a key role in all forms of animal rights in the future. It will surely be the case as well, though, that the all-too-often vague notion of moral rights will be supplemented by more technical, more specific *legal* protections in the form of legal rights and other law-based protections. This trend is likely to, in turn, make use of moral rights all the more common.

What has been the role of the antivivisection movement?

This movement is more than 100 years old, and it was once both the leading edge and most powerful part of the animal protection movement in western cultures. At the end of the nineteenth century in particular, it had great influence in England. Ultimately, it won some battles to limit researchers' use of nonhuman animals, but it ultimately lost the war, in part because Charles Darwin lent his name to the pro-research, anti-protection forces. But the movement produced much good, and today a number of the considerable protections afforded research animals owe their substance and spirit to this important movement. This fact is honored somewhat through continued use of the antiquated term "vivisection" in much animal protection literature.

How significant is today's "alternatives movement"?

The name "alternatives movement" designates the long-standing campaign to replace the use of live animals in research with alternative research methods, or the "3 Rs" approach (replacement, reduction, and refinement). The success of this campaign at the national level in many countries reflects the ethically charged nature of harming a living research subject in order to help some other living being. In the 1960s, both humane organizations and a number of national governments began to fund studies in alternative methods. European governments have invested by far the most resources in this effort. The European Commission in 1992 set up the European Center for the Validation of Alternative Methods, and has since funded it heavily. In the United States, where institutional interest has been significantly lower, the government in 1997 established the Interagency Coordinating Committee on the Validation of Alternative Methods (ICCVAM) to develop and validate new test methods, but this impressive-on-paper effort has not been funded significantly.

Some have argued that a search for alternatives to present approaches unfairly implies criticism of present and past practices. Others have countered that a search for alternatives is, instead, an affirmation of research and science generally, as well as ethical instincts and values.

As to just what "alternatives" involve, the Web site of the industry-funded Center for Alternatives to Animal Testing at Johns Hopkins University in Baltimore, Maryland, explains that the idea of alternatives in animal research is best understood when it is broken down into the subcategories of reduction, refinement, and replacement. Replacement is described as "what most people think of when they think of alternatives.... Studying human or animal cells instead of a whole animal (known as an in vitro method) is an example of a replacement alternative." Another source explains, "A replacement alternative is one that entirely eliminates the need for whole-animal testing."

Reduction alternatives are also described simply: "Just what they sound like: methods that reduce the number of animals necessary for use in a test or experiment." Refinement methods are given an equally commonsense explanation: "Approaches to the use of animals that lessen or eliminate their pain and distress or that ensure more humane endpoints to experiments. For example, choosing an appropriate medication for pain relief following surgery is one type of refinement."

What about public policy? Is there any movement here?

While the official recognition of the alternatives movement in various government policies might be used to suggest that animal protection issues are already part of public policy, this is true in only minor ways. Far more significant is the fact that public policy discussions in most countries remain overwhelmingly human-centered. The assumption that other animals are mere legal things remains the heartbeat of present public policy in both industrialized and developing countries alike. The upshot of this policy approach is that the subordination of any and all nonhuman living beings to human interests of virtually any kind, minor as well as major, remains the working assumption in political discussions.

One might also argue that the emergence of the animal protection successes already mentioned in this book offer hope that policy discussions will not always favor human interests alone. But the demands of competing in an international climate where policy discussions are thoroughly dominated by economics-based analyses are daunting. Public policy toward the poorest in the *human* community reveals the true policies of the industrialized nations. Politicians talk as if the prevailing ideology is that *"all* humans matter." But the realities for many people (especially poor women in rural areas, and certain disfavored ethnic groups that are desperately poor) are that they are ignored and thus their interests unprotected. In a climate where many humans do not have functioning legal protections, it is not surprising that talk about "rights for animals" (meaning, of course, rights for the animals outside the human species) is a low priority for many and derided by leaders who must play to the political forces that keep them in power.

Since the interest of human groups can be ignored easily enough, there is the obvious risk that emerging pro-animal cultural values could easily be subordinated if enough is at stake. The upshot is that the rights and privileges of the richer segments of the human race override nonhuman interests at every turn in ways that are even more virulent and self-serving than the ways the rights of marginalized humans are eclipsed.

Chapter 5 noted that some countries mandate a public policy that engages protections for other animals by mentioning animal protection in their constitutions. In other countries, such as the United Kingdom, animals get on the public policy radar screen through political party programs and the cabinet level of the government. But powerful societies such as the United States and China go forward with public policies that create very stilted senses of "animal protection" for a variety of reasons. In the United States, animal protection remains dominated by an interpretation of the concept of property rights that favors even minor human interests. In China, the ideology of the ruling Communist elite dominates every bit as fully. Thus, while public policy discussions could easily accommodate more openness on animal issues, this is not the case now in some very important circles.

What will be the impact of the increasingly high profile and heavy funding of public health initiatives?

Public health discussions have come to the fore in the last decades, which is laudable because these discussions are focused on prevention of disease rather than only treatment.

But in practice, "public health" discussions are so narrowly focused on human health issues that nonhuman animals are dismissed as unimportant.

The connection between "health," "public," and "animals" is easy to identify—it is the important notion of "zoonotic disease" or "zoonosis," defined generally as a disease that can be transmitted from nonhumans to humans. Cases where humans infect nonhuman animals are referred to as "reverse zoonoses." The root of the word zoonosis is the Greek word *zoon*, "animal." Because humans are as truly members of the "animals" category, as is *any* nonhuman, transmission of disease between humans and nonhumans is basic biological reality. Thus, transmission of diseases from, say, birds to humans is no more astonishing than transmission of diseases between two nonhuman species.

It has been estimated that as many as 75% of the new diseases that have affected humans over the past decade have been caused by pathogens originating from nonhuman animals, in one way or another. These include not only newly emerged diseases, but some older ones as well, usually called reemerging zoonotic diseases. Some of these problems have spread by various means over long distances and become global problems. Even though many zoonoses are preventable (rabies is an example), they cause many deaths and otherwise impact millions of people every year. Tragically, they affect most heavily the poorest segment of the human population. In addition, zoonotic diseases can greatly impact production of food from nonhuman animals. This has created obstacles to national and international trade, and thus drawn the attention of powerful governmental and private interests.

For these reasons, the public health establishment has had an increasingly high profile in policy discussions. The concerns of public health can conflict greatly with concerns for animal protection because of *who* the "public" is when the term "public health" is used. The answer of powerful groups like the Institute of Medicine of the National Academies is that "public" means humans only. Public health is thus defined as "what we, as a society, collectively do to assure the conditions in which *people* can be healthy."

An exclusive focus on humans alone in public health is, as in so many other contexts, counterproductive and ethically narrow. Just as the medical establishment once allocated its resources in narrow ways that focused most heavily on men's medical problems rather than on all humans' problems, today the allocation of public health resources reflects a different narrowness, namely the enactment of multiple measures aimed at prevention of human diseases, even when these measures come at a dreadful cost to entire populations of nonhuman animals.

Human medicine focuses rather naturally on humans, but human-centeredness of this kind in the broader field of public health can be a disaster. As many people know today, human health has long been integrally tied to the health of the more-than-human world. Historically, the spread of disease has played a major role in the expansion of some human civilizations at the expense of others—this is a major point of the best-selling 2005 work of Jared Diamond, *Guns, Germs, and Steel: The Fates of Human Societies.*

When public policy discussions in the area of public health ignore the importance of protecting nonhuman animals and their communities, they set a dangerous precedent. Such human-centeredness distorts our judgments about how to coexist with other animals. These discussions ignore that fact that a heavy concentration on *only* human welfare is very risky in a world that is biologically so intertwined. Further, when humans alone are the focus, it is doubtful that the human community can develop all of humans' rich ethical capacities.

The bottom line is that, while public health discussions now go forward in ways that curtail both moral and legal protections for nonhumans, there is no question but that they can be developed in ways that are respectful of lives beyond the human community. Wildlife matters to the public these days, as measured by important trends like the economic value of wildlife photography and tourism and the fact that so many countries have significantly revised their wildlife legislation and legal frameworks for the protection of wildlife and biodiversity. Such developments are not likely to remain in place unless those involved in public health discussions, including veterinarians, get beyond the humans-only approach.

What is the relationship of animal protection concerns to the worldwide environmental movement?

Environmental concerns have great relevance to animal protection debates because, in practical ways, concerns to protect "the environment" naturally impact both humans and nonhumans alike. Three concerns of the environmental movement are examined here—pollution, extinction, and global warming. There are many more issues of great importance, but these three issues reveal particularly well that the environmental movement and the animal protection movement are at the very least cousins and, even more important, natural allies.

Historically, organizations in these two mega-movements have not worked well together. At times, environmentalists and animal protectionists have confronted each other over issues. The alleged difference between environmentalists and animal protectionists is that the latter are said to look solely at individuals, while the environmentalists looked solely at species. The on-the-ground realities are, in fact, both more subtle and complicated, but it is true that concern for individuals is a major theme and insight of animal protection, just as focus on species-level realities is an important theme and insight in environmental discussions.

But when discussions are framed exclusively in terms of one concern over the other, that is, for the interests or "rights" of *species* as opposed the rights of individual animals, or vice versa, much harm is done. With regard to the debate over which of these two insights is more important, Tom Regan, one of the most famous animal rights philosophers (see chapter 10), suggested species-level concerns amount to "environmental fascism" if and when such a focus overrides individual rights. Any animal protectionist will recognize the insight that drives this observation, but equally, any environmentalist may reply with an even more famous quote from Aldo Leopold, the founder of the environmental movement in the United States. He suggested a principle broader than working on behalf of individuals, namely, working for that which tends "to the good of the biotic community."

Both insights obviously help nonhuman animals. So even if species-level concerns produce thinking and talking that are quite different from the thinking and talking produced by individual-oriented "animal rights" (whether such protections are moral or legal in nature), both approaches produce major benefits for animal protection. Each approach can accommodate insights related to the importance of individuals, just as each approach can incorporate insights about the importance of animals' communities and the welfare of the whole species in relation to other species and the larger habitat or ecosystem.

It is without question, then, that a concern for "the environment" truly opens up many people, including educational and religious communities, to the more-than-human world. But so does a careful study of humans' ethical abilities with the nonhuman animals in and near our own local communities. Both approaches open us up to the world and our own learning about it. It is this feature that means all but the most intractable problems have solutions that can advance the goals of both groups, even if the solution is not fully satisfactory to each side in this potentially dynamic duo.

Concerns for pollution intersect with concerns for nonhuman animals in multiple ways. Chapter 2 mentions the astonishing levels of pollution from food animals. The United Nations 2006 report "Livestock's Long Shadow" connects this pollution to not only the nearby rivers and lakes but also to dead zones in coastal areas and degradation of faraway coral reefs. Further, even as the food animals themselves are impacted by the intensive production methods inside the factory farm, so too are local communities of wildlife (and humans, of course) impacted beyond the borders of the factory farm.

Concern for global warming and climate change have thrust themselves to the fore of our attention and policy discussion in the last five years. The risk here is a familiar one—human-centeredness pursued in ways that eclipse, rather than help us live with, other-than-human communities. Given how inter-woven life on Earth is, it is a biological mistake to pursue an "environmentalism" that is centered on one species. Habitat protection requires biodiversity, and this simple biological fact supports approaches to global warming and other environ-mental issues that are focused not on one species alone but on the health of webs of life.

Does animal protection mean job losses?

Answers to questions about job loss often shape people's will-ingness to consider change on many issues. In animal protection and environmental matters alike, a full and fair answer depends on a number of things, such as which job sector one focuses on, which kinds of protections are put in place, and what kinds of new jobs are created by the protection measures.

If the answer to questions about job losses focuses solely on the group of businesses sometimes lumped together as "animal use industries," the answer is surely that some jobs will be lost if the animal protection measures eliminate present practices and no replacement industries are created. So if factory farms and their large slaughterhouses are eliminated, the jobs within them will obviously be lost. But if people raise meat or produce or process high-protein alternatives locally, or if consultants, spe-cialists, and others have new employment and business opportu-nities that fill the vacuum, then replacement jobs will be created.

Importantly, even though the deeper issues are the question of *net* job losses across modern economies generally and the quality of jobs lost versus the quality of those that replace them, the loss of specific people's jobs remains an important topic to address with candor and sensitivity. The solution lies in creating meaningful jobs that are sustainable well into the future.

This is no simple task. Those who advocate abolition of the use of animals for meat, for example, propose a solution that will greatly impact the poor around the world. The FAO's 2006 report estimates that around the world as many as 987 million *poor people* are involved in raising livestock. Human ingenuity and ethical sensibilities need to address all the animals—human and nonhuman alike—that animal protection measures impact.

In the 1970s, advocates of saving a minnow-size fish known as the snail darter, which was believed to be on the brink of oblivion, blocked an agency of the United States government from building a huge dam. The case went to the Supreme Court, which sided with the fish, but the United States Congress then intervened to override protection of the small fish. The obscurity of the animals involved, as well as their peculiar name, created much skepticism about both environmental and animal protection. Later, a campaign to protect forests which were necessary for the survival of an obscure owl became controversial in the American Northwest because job losses were affected if logging was curtailed.

Both cases leave no doubt that protection of nonhuman animals can lead to important economic changes that involve immediate job losses and other economic consequences. The fact that such consequences are not uncommon when legal protections are expanded does not make the threatened changes and job losses easier to accept. Expansion of legal protection in favor of one group (whether human or not) often means that the privileges of another group will be contracted.

There are now economists who look at the larger picture, for it can clearly be the case that animal protection measures produce net economic benefits. Important issues include the quality of life for the slaughterhouse workers whose problems are mentioned in chapter 2. Of great importance as well is the conclusion of the Pew/Johns Hopkins report described in chapter 2 that factory farming is not helpful economically to local communities.

A key in going forward is finding solutions that respect both human and nonhuman community concerns, rather than simply resolving issues in ways that protect existing jobs. There are well-documented cases in which animal protection measures led to job losses but ultimately created many more jobs—perhaps the best-known example is termination of whaling, which was followed by development of a whale-watching industry that provided far more sustainable jobs in the end.

What impact do ethnic and national food traditions have on animal rights discussions?

In psychologically deep ways, traditional values attached to inherited food practices greatly impact individual choices. Food traditions confer identity, are the anchors of many family and holiday celebrations, and are often associated with religious convictions and ethnic pride. National holidays, when different meats like lamb, turkey, pork, goat, or fish are often the centerpiece of a meal, can also function in this way.

The deep psychological dimensions of eating animals and the practices by which food animals are brought to meals have led to traditions that have been central in every culture. It has been estimated that for 99% of the time during which the human species has existed, hunting other animals for food was an integral part of humans' existence, supplementing what could be gathered from one's local area. Because both gathering and hunting produced essential nutrients and materials and thus were necessary in many places for biological survival, both became integral parts of daily, and eventually cultural, life. Hunting also led many cultures to learn about and, most often, to have a deep respect for other animals. This fact is reflected in the attitudes toward animals reflected in indigenous peoples' worldviews.

Because traditions that draw their energies from ethnic identity or a national or religious food tradition are among the deepest psychological anchors for many humans, those who challenge the unseen production practices that make meat available for culturally significant meals often face insurmountable obstacles. But it has clearly been the case that some traditional practices can be so harmful to the food animals that concerned citizens seek to modify the recurring harms that these culinary traditions hold in place. Such challenges sometimes have attempted to change the underlying production practices, while at other times the approach has been to alter the consumption habits of those who inherited the harmful tradition.

But just as past challenges to many human-on-human oppressions have revealed again and again that those who benefit from an oppression will hold tenaciously to their inherited traditions and practices, so too have animal activists learned the lesson that challenging traditional food practices is not for the faint of heart. Those who challenge such practices need strategies for protecting the core values of those people whose practices are being challenged. These strategies have included invoking the important animal protection values also found in the ethnic or religious tradition involved (an example using this strategy in Islam is given in chapter 1). Sometimes the actual act of killing has been replaced by a symbolic act. Such strategies seek a culturally meaningful alternative, because such a solution can be perceived as coming from within the tradition itself and thus avoiding the problems any group has when outsiders presume to impose foreign values on the group's inherited practices.

What role do religious traditions play in the politics of animal protection?

As suggested repeatedly in this book, religious beliefs and practices shape many people's willingness or refusal to consider animal protections. Every religious tradition reflects the insight that harming other living beings presents problems. In the Jewish tradition, a concern for the suffering of all living beings is among the most ancient of that tradition's teachings.

In Christianity's Catholic tradition, images of Saint Francis of Assisi, known for preaching to the birds, are among the most common in local churches. In the Islamic Qur'an, a well-known passage observes, "There is not a thing that moves on the earth, no bird that flies on its wings, but has a community of its own like yours." In the Hindu, Buddhist and Jain communities throughout the world, the principle of *ahimsa*, or "not harming," is taught as among humans' most important ethical and religious duties and applies as fully to nonhumans as it does to humans. The Chinese traditions also offer a worldview that presupposes values and ethics that can be very friendly and liberating for nonhuman animals.

In important areas like husbandry and slaughter, religious traditions were the original sources of humane principles. For example, both the Jewish and Islamic traditions originated rules that required the person killing an animal to be specially trained and to kill the animal as quickly and humanely as possible.

But if religions have contributed awareness of the importance of not harming other living beings, they have also featured practices and explanations that subordinate other living beings to human life. Some religious traditions today still mandate the slaughter of huge numbers of animals, while food practices are often frozen in place by explicitly religious justifications that do not permit any change, even when the proposed change is consistent with the tradition's own original insight that humane slaughter is an important goal.

Changing harmful practices can be extremely difficult because practices are often centuries, even millennia old. Some are anchored in scriptures considered revealed down to even the tiniest detail. Further, many religious adherents are expressly taught that "animals are for humans." Nonetheless, every religious tradition (though not every sub-tradition or narrow fundamentalist version of the larger tradition) offers important current developments and future possibilities for animal protection and the deeply spiritual senses of animal rights.

7

SOCIAL REALITIES

In the daily lives of humans are many opportunities to protect or harm nonhuman animals. Through consumer choices, environmentally sensitive acts, or treatment of nearby animals, individual humans create animal protections or harms. For this reason, social realities are as important as are the policy decisions that take place in political circles.

What are the prevailing attitudes today in different societies regarding animals?

Attitudes around the world reveal that four different themes are now prevailing. Each country weaves these themes into a unique pattern depending upon cultural, religious, and political variables. It is not unusual, then, to find in a particular society that one of these themes is far more prominent than the other three themes. But if one looks closely enough, virtually all societies today reflect all four of these themes.

The first theme is diversity of attitudes, which has been mentioned as occurring in many societies and cultures. The second theme is change, which is grounded in the fact that societies around the globe are in deep ferment over our relationships with other living beings. The third theme is the continuing influence of traditional or inherited values, for these play an important part in the way people talk about the final theme, which is the rich set of possibilities for the future of human-animal relationships.

The *diversity* theme is, for obvious reasons, not easy to summarize in a few sentences. There is one level of diversity at the international level when one compares one society to another. In one sense, this book is a recitation of the incredibly wide range of attitudes one finds as one moves from society to society around the world.

Diversity *within* each society is also a particularly striking phenomenon. The best evidence of diversity is familiarity with the grassroots elements that attempt protection at the local level of individual animals, wildlife communities, and environmentally important approaches like habitat preservation, reclamation, and restoration. This work takes a secular form in some places and religious forms in others.

Diversity of both the internal and international kinds is expressed in educational practices, legal approaches, and religious attitudes. One often finds some form of animal protection at the level of formal government rule, but even more commonly one finds animal protection in daily life and informal social ethics.

The theme of *change* or ferment arises in many different contexts in this volume. This phenomenon deepens the existing diversity and also challenges many people because of the psychological force of inherited ideas in human cultures.

The third theme—*tradition,* or inherited practices and attitudes toward other living beings—is discussed in the following section. The final theme is *future possibilities* regarding how humans will live their lives on a planet that is also home to an astonishing array of nonhuman animals. This is an ancient theme, having been announced in every religion around the world, and yet it is a new and renewing theme today sounded in many ways throughout the educational, legal, and scientific establishments of societies around the world.

In each country, these four themes are constantly rewoven in culturally distinct ways as they grow and change. The result is ever-growing ferment in attitudes in most societies and across the world.

What is our heritage?

Because humans are traditional and culture-rich animals, each individual's heritage can come from family, teachers outside the family, the community and its institutions, and especially from one's culture and its religious traditions. These diverse sources can reinforce each other or be in marked tension with one another. When one recognizes as well that cultural attitudes of many societies often feature deep traditions of compassion alongside customs of eating, hunting, and otherwise using certain work or game animals, the result is a rich tapestry of options.

Cultural and familial heritages are major factors when one asks people why they believe and act as they do in matters involving our inevitable intersection with life beyond our own species. Some traditions have long favored protection of all living beings—a well-known example is the Jain community in India. Other communities, as noted in many sections of this book, have animal use traditions that are central to cultural or tribal identity. Vegetarian communities exist in many Hindu and Buddhist societies, and while there are fewer in the Jewish, Christian, and Islamic religions, vegetarian traditions have long had a place there as well.

Given the present predicament of nonhuman animal communities around the world, it obviously remains true that many traditions feature claims about the supremacy of humans. For a variety of reasons, people think of their inherited traditions as a birthright or legacy that honors the past. For example, hunting traditions within a family or community or culture are often thought of as a form of sharing with one's remote ancestors or one's own parents and grandparents. Such traditions can come in forms that are deeply respectful of life (this is often the case with indigenous groups that still hunt), but hunting traditions can also degenerate into disrespectful exercises, an example of which is "canned hunting" where hunters pay to shoot penned animals that have no chance whatsoever of escape.

Some traditional claims for humans' superiority are so thoroughgoing and radical that followers of that tradition are psychologically predisposed to dismiss animal protection as a modern innovation and an alien imposition from outsiders. It is nonetheless the case that virtually every tradition has historical features that do pertain to the importance of animal protection, even if these features have been forgotten or rationalized away by today's cultural leaders. A good example is the ethic of kindness and compassion that every cultural tradition has developed in some way or another. These in particular continue to have powerful psychological dimensions for many people today.

The heritage of many people today is thus mixed. For a variety of reasons, dismissals of animal protection are likely to remain prominent in many countries, even as young people and others promote animal protection causes. As discussed often in this book, in a world where women, ethnic groups, and immigrants are often subordinated as citizens of one country or another, it is to be expected that subordination of nonhuman animals is but one problem among others.

What importance have compassion and anticruelty had in the past?

Concern for others is such an ancient theme that scholars often have identified it with the very beginning of religion. The best-selling scholar Karen Armstrong in her 2006 book *The Great Transformation* observed how care about all living beings became a hallmark of the important time in prehistory called "the axial age." During the period from 900 B.C.E. to 200 B.C.E., ancient religious sages in China, India, Israel, and Greece taught that "your concern must somehow extend to the entire world...Each tradition developed its own formulation of the Golden Rule: do not do to others what you would not have done to you. As far as the Axial sages were concerned, respect for the sacred rights of *all beings*—not orthodox belief—was religion."

This is why one finds many examples of animal-friendly quotes in the Old Testament, ancient Chinese texts, the scriptures of India, and the earliest Greek thinkers. The compassion found in these earliest traditions continued to play an important part and even to blossom further in the Qur'an, writings of early Christian leaders, later Buddhist scriptures, and the lives of many religious figures.

As described in chapter 6, it is true that religious institutions often led their traditions toward forms of human-centeredness that obscured these ancient beginnings. Nonetheless, there are many examples of later believers finding compassion for all beings to be a key to the religious life. One of the earliest examples of an anticruelty law was passed in 1641 by the Puritans in the Massachusetts colony in North America: "No man shall exercise any Tirranny or Crueltie towards any bruite Creature which are usuallie kept for man's use." In many societies, the power of the compassion tradition was such that scriptural provisions exhorting respect for other life ensured that the compassion tradition would continually remain a part of the religious heritage.

In secular realms, civil law became an important carrier that kept compassion sentiments among social values. In England, the 1822 legislation known as Martin's Law was supported not only by prominent Christians but by many others as well.

In the small-scale societies that we often call "indigenous peoples," insights about the importance of ethical action toward all living beings are reflected in many unique ways. These societies reflect well that each group of people has used human imagination to integrate animal protection customs into their education, culture, and daily life.

That every society has had both anticruelty provisions and also other positive teachings providing respect for nonhuman animals reflects how common, natural, and truly human are protective attitudes toward other living beings. This is one reason that there are so many manifestations of concern for both human and nonhuman animals today. Because human-centeredness has sometimes reached such a fever pitch that compassion issues are subordinated, as is the case with modern production of meat, the predictable reaction has been a worldwide social movement to reinstate compassion as a leading human virtue.

Put this all together and one gets an "animal rights" movement that promotes an ethic of kindness and concern, that opposes the kinds of cruelty that one finds in modern practices like factory farming, use of other living beings as research tools, the killing of unwanted dogs and cats, and the decimation of wildlife through habitat destruction. Today, societies around the world are not only concerning themselves with the individual who commits cruelty but also with government agencies and businesses that do not factor compassion into their policies and practices.

How are attitudes changing today?

This book describes a diverse range of developments that reflect two changes that combine to produce today's ferment on animal issues. First, more and more people are aware today that dismissive and disrespectful attitudes toward living beings outside our own species have had harmful effects, and thus such attitudes are being challenged in almost countless ways. Second, as an array of challenges develops to harmful practices and attitudes, people recognize that they must now choose how to interact with other living beings.

An obvious but almost always impractical option is to reinstate ancient views. A more realistic option is to incorporate ancient insights about the importance of respect for other living beings with more modern insights from science about the animals that live nearby.

Recognition of existing problems in how other animals are treated has, along with appreciation of new possibilities, prompted much coverage of animal issues in the media and in education. There is also much more discussion of the ways in which consumer choices and eating options might be adjusted. Administrators and students in local schools, community activists who create nonprofit organizations, the leaders of religious communities, and elders in their own groups are prompting private and governmental institutions at the local levels and beyond to become involved in animal care, spay and neuter programs, wildlife protection, discussion of food production, environmental programs, and much else.

All of these efforts combine to increase the willingness of citizens to listen and discuss options. This in turn opens up the animal question in community after community. Such grassroots developments stimulate the human imagination to ever more creativity. This is the key mechanism in leading our society, its governmental institutions, and the private sectors of our society to approach animal issues with sensitivity. Finally, such changes make the following question a key issue as problem after problem is addressed.

How well informed are modern consumers about current practices regarding animals?

A common story circulated among animal protectionists involves a family member or friend who responds "I don't want to know" as they hear about one problem or another with nonhuman animals. It is the case that many consumers do not care to know about the harms that are integral parts of modern production practices. This is also true of many products that involve oppression of humans.

It is nonetheless true today, however, that awareness of the basic facts of many modern problems is increasing. An example is modern food production, where confinement, separation of offspring from mother, and slaughter are ugly realities that prompt more and more comment and involvement. The Internet has provided an inexpensive and efficient source of spreading information and images worldwide, as well as updates on alternative products.

What makes this trend important is that, by and large, disclosure about the conditions within which animal products are created is *not* mandated by law. But the prevalence of terms such as "cruelty free," "not tested on animals," "free range," and "humane certified" testify to the fact that many efforts are under way to provide options for consumers so that they can avoid supporting harmful practices that many producers prefer to hide.

As younger people who are exposed to open-minded inquiries about production realities come of age, they will make the power of engaged consumers a constant force in social policy regarding how we treat other living beings. This power is summed up nicely by Frances Moore Lappe's observation that "every choice we make can be a celebration of the world we want."

What about circuses and zoos? Do they educate us or imprison us?

It is increasingly common to see certain practices controlled or even banned by local, regional, or even national governments—a good example is the 2009 vote by the Bolivian government to outlaw the use of wild and domestic animals in circuses. Hundreds of communities around the world now have bans in place on circus practices because the traditional circus transports, houses, and treats many animals, such as tigers, elephants, and even dolphins, in completely unsatisfactory ways. This commercial enterprise often cloaks itself in claims about "education," but the realities are that profit-oriented motives drive this formerly popular, even if often cruel form of entertainment. Bans of harmful practices at local levels create powerful muscles that can grow well beyond local communities to regional, province-wide, national, and even international discussions.

Zoos have also been an area where the ferment over human treatment of nonhumans has created pressures on modern institutions. The idealized image that zoos project today is quite different from the historical realities of zoos. Zoos are an ancient institution among humans, dating back to at least the third millennium B.C.E. They have thus long been a part of the human landscape. They occurred in ancient Egypt, China, Mesopotamia, Greece, Italy, and Mexico. As noted in chapter 2, notoriously harsh and destructive practices based on the exhibition of animals took place in ancient Rome, where thousands upon thousands of animals were slaughtered for entertainment purposes.

By some measures, zoos flourish today; in Britain alone there are more than 100 collections of animals to choose from, while in the United States they number in the many hundreds. Today's zoos are heirs to trends first evident in the late nineteenth and early twentieth centuries. These helped zoos develop occasional sensitivity to appalling conditions of captivity, although only a few of the major institutions carried out projects which provided animals with anything like a natural or satisfactory habitat. The twentieth century saw an increased awareness of both the technical problems and moral issues of animals that must live in artificial communities.

Controversy over the propriety of zoos themselves arose as early as the eighteenth century in England and France. Many have attempted to justify the existence of zoos on educational grounds. Some have also asserted that zoos are needed because of the roles zoos are said to play in the conservation and preservation of species threatened by humans, but there remains controversy over the effectiveness of zoos in conservation efforts.

The poor conditions that prevailed for so long in early zoos continue today in many places. In those modern zoos which are acknowledged as the world's finest, problem situations remain but are confined to fewer and fewer species. Modern zoo keeping, especially as it is reflected in textbooks, is sensitive to this problem and continues to strive for improvements. The competition among zoos for tourist revenues remains a factor in the management of today's zoos. In an unfortunate way, this can contribute to the demand for exotic animals to be exhibited. This in turn helps drive the market for captured wild animals. Zoos may publicly deride the horrible practices of capture and transport, but they sometimes contribute indirectly to these realities.

Despite the fact that zoo representatives aggressively claim new functions for zoos, including education, conservation, and management, the realities for the captive animals remain very tough. Thus, although some zoo advocates claim that it is one of the most important roles of zoos to motivate the public to take action, the action to be taken is never about the propriety of zoo captivity itself, which clearly raises ethical questions that interest many. Instead, zoos attempt to prompt work to improve the conditions of free-living populations of wild animals. This is one reason that critics continue to challenge the *actual*, on-the-ground realities in even the best-managed zoos.

Particularly challenging is the long-standing practice of holding large, intelligent, socially complex animals such as elephants, nonhuman primates, and members of many dolphin species. Studies show that many large animals, such as elephants and the large cats, need much more room than zoos can provide. The small size of enclosures and other features of even the best zoos create what critics call "anthropogenic," or human-caused problems, such as foot injuries that plague elephants in captivity but which are rare in the wild. Creative studies about trauma in other animals suggest that captivity itself can have altogether negative impacts on individuals—a good example can be found in Gay Bradshaw's essay regarding trauma in elephants in the 2008 collection titled *An Elephant in the Room: The Science and Well-being of Elephants in Captivity.*

So if zoos are serious about their announced intention to contribute to the existence of healthy, well-managed captive populations, they must go beyond their claim that they can exhibit any and all nonhuman animals for public education and scientific study. Zoos have yet to answer what amounts to the most basic of animal rights inquiries, namely, whether there will ever be a time when the zoo establishment recommends that captivity is, for ethical reasons, wrong for *some* animals. Modern science has made it clear that some animals simply do not belong in captivity because they, like humans, are so complex mentally and socially that they suffer when in captivity, even if kept healthy and well fed. Captivity itself thus raises fundamental issues that must be distinguished from technical problems, such as the inability to get some kinds of animals to reproduce in captive circumstances. Rather, this particular question focuses on *ethical* or *moral* abilities that make humans special.

Many groups focus on specific animals. There are protection groups that insist that nonhuman great apes (gorillas, chimpanzees, orangutans, and bonobos) cannot be kept in captivity in ethically honest ways because evidence of these animals' day-to-day realities is that they suffer and are, like humans, such complex individuals that they should never be treated as property. Others have made similar moral arguments on behalf of elephants, which suffer dramatically when we hold them captive. A rich set of arguments has also been made on behalf of orcas, bottlenose dolphins, and any number of other kinds of dolphins and porpoises—they are simply too complex to thrive in captivity. Advocates for these animals and others simply too complex to thrive in zoos are almost always willing to make exceptions based on self-defense or public safety considerations. But such problems are individual-level considerations and can be handled much as we handle similar problems caused by certain humans.

This kind of argument prompts the question of whether zoos imprison *us*, that is, they lock us and our children into a mentality of domination that, in the end, is detrimental, creating terrible harms for the animals that we use for entertainment, profit, and education. One reason this is a risk is that the claimed educational functions of zoos are not nearly as simple as zoos portray them. Many children recognize that despite zoos' "educational" messages, our society approves of the captivity of other animals for our entertainment. What makes it fair to ask if zoos imprison us is that zoos acknowledge in their conservation materials what everyone knows, namely, the best place for some animals is not in our zoos but in their natural setting amid their social groups, living a free life.

The alleged educational "benefits" of our captivity traditions have thus been thrown open to discussion today. The very holding of large, sentient creatures in captivity is seen to open up a range of questions about true, quality education and the importance of clearly distinguishing that important goal from both mere entertainment and the income-making potential of captive animal exhibitions.

What is the role of sanctuaries?

There are an increasing number of specially designed refuges that many different people and organizations have created as one way to offer short-term solutions for severe problems. While placing animals in a sanctuary is not the same as setting the animals free, the very notion of "sanctuary" implies safety. What complicates matters from an ethical standpoint is that sanctuaries characteristically were formed out of necessity to house animals formerly held in traditional forms of harmful captivity. Because sanctuaries try to minimize, if not eliminate, suffering of their animals, they characteristically describe their mission as focused on the welfare of each individual animal. At times they also blend in commitments to education elements or conservation efforts.

Sanctuaries, which in practice are quite diverse, attempt this idealistic mission in a wide variety of ways because they have limited funds and land. Ideally, sanctuaries strive to put their captive animals in environments that are natural, spacious, and enriched to provide for both the individual and social needs of the animals. But practical realities of limited space and money often limit greatly what can be done for the animals.

The very nature of the sanctuary enterprise, then, presents major challenges. Providing care to animals held captive before arriving at the sanctuary is a challenge because prior care often has been poor. When animals need to be moved to sanctuaries it is because they have not been in optimum environments. Sanctuaries are further challenged to provide care for their captive animals through all stages of life, to address behavioral abnormalities, and to attend to individual needs while also considering the impact on the whole sanctuary community. Often sanctuaries euthanize when the quality of life of an animal deteriorates (in the opinion of the sanctuary managers) to the point where death is in the best interest of the suffering animal.

Housing large dangerous animals, such as elephants that suffered in zoos or circuses, or providing refuge for non-human primates after years in laboratories, or giving farm animals a full life after their most productive years have passed—all of these have their obvious challenges and financial obligations.

A key difference between sanctuaries and zoos is zoos' major emphasis on the necessity of breeding in order to ensure the existence of a sustainable captive population. Sanctuaries, on the other hand, oppose breeding as morally wrong, just as they typically oppose the idea of maintaining captive populations in general. But preventing animals in sanctuaries from reproducing is also an issue, for it raises both practical problems and ethical questions about the right of humans to deny reproduction, even if that helps eliminate the perpetuation of captivity for future generations.

What animals are in the city?

While a common belief in many industrialized nations is that "animals" other than companion animals, research animals, and zoo animals live out beyond the city limits, modern research shows that even intense urban environments have a surprising amount of nonhuman life in their midst. These include many birds, various rodents and other small mammals, a variety of reptiles, and a wide range of insects and other creatures that fall beneath humans' notice.

Some cities tolerate much larger wildlife—the classic example is India, where the "sacred cow" is a common site in many urban settings. In some cities, one form or another of wildlife can become a tourist attraction. One well-known example was the red-tailed hawk named Pale Male that lived on a window ledge high above New York City's Central Park. Another well-known individual was Pelorus Jack, a Risso's dolphin who between 1888 and 1912 became a celebrity by companioning ships through Cook Strait in New Zealand.

When nonhumans share urban and suburban environments with humans, there are inevitably major issues of several kinds. Companion animals, for example, are quite visible in modern cities as humans exercise these animals. But less visible are the colonies of feral cats that exist in the margins of many city spaces, even in climates with cold winters. Feral dogs are more visible as they roam cities in more temperate climates. Wildlife in the most intense urban environments includes the species mentioned above, but suburban environments of Europe and North America are rich with a wide variety of birds, deer, coyotes and foxes, beaver, and even bears and moose. These urban dwellers offer the opportunity for urban and local communities to handle more than the usual set of issues raised by companion animals, such as cosmetic surgery bans, leash laws, breed bans, and spay/neuter programs. Truly free-living wildlife and feral animal colonies challenge communities to identify future possibilities for living with nonhuman animals.

8

EDUCATION, THE
PROFESSIONS, AND THE ARTS

Education, the professions, and the arts have all been a rich part of human ingenuity. Each has also played important roles in humans' past interactions with other living beings, and each will surely play such roles in future possibilities.

The "education" examined here is school-based education. This is the most formal sort of education, and in fundamental ways it is different from the "education" that zoos claim as the result of their exhibition of captive animals. This formal education is also different from the more immediate, hands-on education one derives from spending considerable time in the field with animals in their environment. While the remarkable benefits that one gets from familiarity with actual animals as they live and thrive in their own communities can be pursued in a variety of ways, this approach happens relatively infrequently in education premised primarily on books, classroom discussions, and controlled experiments at the laboratory bench. Characteristically, in such formal education, the emphasis is on ideas from the fields we call "the humanities" (sometimes the "arts and humanities"), "the social sciences," and the different endeavors we divide up as "the natural sciences."

Education of this formal kind is a latecomer to studies about nonhuman animals, and surprisingly its overall features make it none too friendly to concerns for nonhuman animals. Some educators, such as those in the veterinary profession discussed below, have been reluctant to embrace animal rights, while other educators, such as the philosophers described in chapters 3 and 10, have taken leading roles in the modern animal rights movement. Overall, though, the larger education system has only slowly become aware of the importance of learning about animals. In this it contrasts with some of the arts discussed briefly at the end of this section.

What is the most effective way of learning about animals?

Although it is obvious that the commonsense approach of learning about a particular animal in the presence of that animal has undeniable value, this is far less common than one might think. Consider the principal ways that children learn about animals. They learn about animals from various authorities, beginning with parents and older members of their extended families. They learn from teachers in school how certain animals act and which animals matter to the human community. If the child attends religious ceremonies in his or her community of faith, the child learns from the leaders of that local community about the relationship of humans to other living beings.

Some children learn in the presence of dogs and cats, or around farm animals. But many children learn only in the abstract about "animals." For example, many children learn about animals primarily from simplified stories drawn from their culture—in a western culture the stories might be drawn from television cartoons or, if the child is educated in a traditional way, from Aesop's fables or the fairy tales of Hans Christian Andersen. In India the stories might be drawn from ancient folk story collections, an example of which is the Jataka tales dealing with the previous lives of the Buddha in the guise of many different kinds of nonhuman animals before finally being reborn as a human.

Juveniles and young adults can learn from experience with particular animals, of course, but since so many people now live fully urban and suburban lives, it is far more common that juveniles and teenagers learn the lore passed along by their schoolteachers, the media, neighbors, and other community members. Many thus learn about different animals not in the presence of those animals but as a part of learning to speak and read as a member of their culture. Gradually, most people take on the prevailing story that their birth culture tells about the living beings beyond our own species. These stories are told—inculcated, really—in a thousand different ways.

Speakers of the English language, for example, learn through constant use of the phrase "humans and animals" to distinguish humans from all other living beings. Humans may or may not technically be described as animals in the later stages of formal education (as in biology classes or in a philosophy course), but in the earliest stages dominated by stories, nationalism, religion, and fairy tales, the division between humans and other living beings becomes an integral part of each student's worldview.

Not all cultures have talked in this way, and especially not in ways that decisively remove humans from the community of the rest of life. Some children learn a culture story that puts humans squarely amid the larger community of life. But today in industrialized cultures the custom of talking about humans as distinct from animals is a dominant theme, and accordingly most children, juveniles, adults, and the elderly live their lives convinced that humans are not only a distinct species but even a separate category of life, entirely unlike all other animals. This is a result of the fact that modern institutions, including those that dominate education, the professions, and the arts, promote in countless ways the notion that humans are separate from the rest of the animal world.

The result is that virtually all of education about animals leaves modern people poorly informed about other animals.

This is one reason that so many political discussions, public policies, laws, religions, and educational approaches treat the customary division "humans and animals" as if it is a natural divide rather than merely a custom masquerading as the order of nature.

At the same time, there are other educators who provide a different point of view. Some people learn to notice other animals and take them seriously. They prompt learning from the animals themselves, or learning at the feet of those who have had significant experience with nonhuman animals. No one disputes that learning about horses, for example, can be altogether richer when it is stimulated by people who have spent a lifetime around horses. Similarly, when learning about fish or orcas or elephants or wolves is guided by people who have lived for decades in the vicinity of such animals and take them seriously, the result is education of a surpassing quality.

All of these forms of learning—school-based, culture-based, animal-based—can be supplemented by personal reflection, travel in other countries and cultures, and the insights of others we come across in education, media, and friendships. This is an important additional process, particularly when one recognizes that social and cultural values about humans in relationship with other living beings are today being reexamined. When reflection is brought to bear on human-animal relationships, and the realities of the animals are considered, those who care enough to notice other animals and then take them seriously have the benefit of unlearning stereotypes and dismissals. But sometimes we are born into times where such freedoms are not possible. Sometimes we attend schools where students are given good grades for rote learning and affirming standard stereotypes.

We return later in this chapter to the issue of what children know about other animals. Interestingly, many adults who are today between the ages of 40 and 70 cite surprisingly often that conversations with their children provided one way they opened up to "animal issues."

What has been the traditional role of animals in education?

In education that is rigidly tied to the classroom setting and to books from past authorities, the traditional role of nonhuman animals in education has been minor. It has been accomplished via images, not emphases on the animals themselves. Even when some biological beings themselves are considered, they are often animals that have been radically subordinated to humans, such as companion and farm animals. Nonhuman animals also populate stories where they demonstrate morals geared to human situations and act as "pets" that come and go in childhood. Such methods reinforce the prevailing attitudes in today's educational institutions about humans' superiority to all other animals.

Have compassion and anticruelty been important values in education?

Given that, as noted in chapter 7, every society has recognized the importance of both compassion and anticruelty concerns, and given that teachings on these subjects appear in the Bible, the Qu'ran, the voluminous scriptures from India and China, and every folktale collection, the answer to this question is, without question, yes.

Many educational institutions mandate teaching of "humane education," although some developments suggest that humane education is being marginalized because of budget pressures and thus not taught broadly or in any serious way. The nineteenth century saw a push to get the subject of humane principles taught in school. Today humane education requirements are often "on the books" but not funded by legislatures for a variety of reasons. One of the less controversial forms of "animal rights" is working to ensure funding of existing requirements that humane education be taught.

But one fairly asks what the real education is in teaching students generalities about the importance of being "humane," even as they are fed factory-farmed food or taken to visit zoos. The deeper educational message, as pointed out in chapter 7, is that nonhuman animals are rightfully subordinated to humans, who alone are the really important beings. Nonetheless, students often come to the conclusion that meat production can be inhumane, or that captive animals in zoos are not nearly as free as the term "wildlife" implies.

What is happening in earliest (elementary) levels of education?

The elementary level reflects some of the most fundamental changes in teaching about animals, and also teaching with animals, in modern schools. This development is not a matter of curricular philosophy as much as it is a matter of children's fascination with other living beings, which gives the topic "animals" simply remarkable educational value for children. To understand why this is so, it helps to watch children in the presence of animals. Alternatively, when visiting a children's bookstore, notice how common are animal images (that is, images of animals other than humans) on covers and pages of, literally, *hundreds upon hundreds* of books. Even an informal review will suggest that nonhuman animal images are by a considerable measure the most common type of images used in children's literature.

The prevalence and importance of these images stems from the fact that children have a deep, natural affinity for other animals. Today there is an ongoing revolution in the study of children's relationships with other animals, and this change in thinking has led to much more openness about why animal issues are so important at the earliest levels of formal education.

Children's fascination with other living beings occurs for some very interesting reasons only recently well understood. Many educators today recognize that both adults and key child psychologists have long misgauged children's interactions with other animals. Books such as Gene Myers's 1998 *Children and Animals: Social Development and Our Connection to Other*

Species and Gail Melson's *Why the Wild Things Are: Animals in the Lives of Children* (2001) have helped educators better understand the importance of children's natural curiosity about and connection to other living beings. Melson has observed that "children's ties to animals seem to have slipped below the radar screens of almost all scholars of child development." With sensitivity to these ties, pioneering humans have been able to develop therapies based on the power some other animals have to affect emotionally troubled children.

A second insight is related. Cognitive psychologists have discovered that children develop early in their lives what some have called a "naïve biology" or, to use Melson's description, "a core domain of knowledge about living things." Careful study reveals that this feature of children's engagement with the world begins to grow in infancy. By preschool years, as Melson observes, "this knowledge base, particularly about animals, already is well established."

A related insight is recognition of the unfortunate habit of dismissing children's natural affinity for other animals. This is being rectified in education today at the primary level. In the past, children were often compared to other animals for negative reasons. The psychologist G. Stanley Hall said in 1904, "To the young child, there is no gap between his soul and that of animals." This comparison was negative, for other animals were considered then to be immoral and without significant intelligence. Only when children emerged into adulthood, shedding concern for "animals," were they considered to be "mature." But as Melson points out, while many other cultures "recognize the affinity of children for animals and build on its images that link children to animals," modern industrialized cultures work to undo this affinity. "At the same time, children in Western cultures gradually absorb a worldview of humans as radically distinct from and superior to other species, the human as 'top dog' in the evolutionary chain of being. What [Myers] calls 'the categorically human self' emerges—a strict division between human attributes and often negatively valued animal characteristics." This facile dismissal of children's affinities is being rectified in some circles of primary education today.

The association of children with animals has had some beneficial effects, fortunately. In the late nineteenth century, the rescue in New York City of an abused child was significantly aided by the existence of anticruelty statutes that protected *other animals*. This is the famous Mary Ellen case covered heavily at the time by the media, which in the nineteenth century often referred to children as "human animals" who were as worthy of protection as were horses and dogs. Humane literature of the period also described children as "little animals" because they were, like the nonhuman animals benefitting from the then-ascendant anticruelty movement, "innocent" and therefore richly deserving of fundamental protections.

A fourth and final insight related to education today at the primary level is bias inherent in characterizing indigenous peoples as not only childish, because of their deep connections to other animals, but also as simple, naïve, and less than sophisticated. Words such as "savage" (which comes originally from the word for forest and was originally a reference to non-city people) and "primitives" have been used to demean people of disfavored cultures. Ironically, indigenous peoples are quite sophisticated in many matters, and certainly often more so than today's urbanized citizens when it comes to knowledge of nonhuman animals' behavior. The dismissal of these peoples and their cultural achievements from the eighteenth century through today has been both self-serving and ignorance-driven.

Educational practices based on these insights offer the prospect of an upcoming generation far more open to humans living in a mixed community shared with many other forms of life. What makes this possible is that children today often alert their parents to the importance of nonhuman animals, such that many people in business, law, education, and government are more aware of the moral nature of concerns for animals and have even taken on animal-sensitive viewpoints because of their children's interests. Such viewpoints can easily go under a variety of names, from "animal rights," compassion, and anticruelty to a concern for the larger community of life and living sustainably in a shared environment.

There are important areas of dispute over animal issues that arise in children's lives. The principal way that many children encounter other animals in their schools is on their lunch plate. Who decides what children eat is an important subject, and there are many educational institutions where conversations are now ongoing about whether children should be afforded a choice in what they eat while at school.

The English philosopher Mary Midgley suggested that "animals, like song and dance, are an innate taste" and we, as humans, are members of a "mixed community." Children can, if we notice them and take them seriously, reteach us open-mindedness regarding the nonhuman living beings in this mixed community.

What about secondary education (pre-college education)?

Students who have entered the stage of formal education before college, variously called by names like "secondary education" and "high school," today reflect much interest in not only non-human animals but also in both the moral and legal senses of "animal rights." The concern is sometimes expressed as a desire to be a veterinarian or "like Jane Goodall" because this well-known primatologist represents both healing of animals and caring discovery about them as members of their own communities. For this reason, the list of student organizations in schools at this level in thousands upon thousands of instances includes an "animal rights club" or its equivalent.

A particularly complex topic at this level is known as "dissection choice." A traditional activity in biology classes has been dissection of various living beings ranging from worms to frogs to small mammals. Some students have refused this exercise on the grounds of conscience, and this has led to major educational and legal disputes over the right of children to make such choices.

The competing arguments in this area focus on different priorities. The argument against giving students the right to opt out of such an exercise suggests that such an option has two negative effects. The first negative affect, it is argued, is that such a choice undermines science. One shortcoming in this argument is that not every student will end up doing science. Another shortcoming is that a student's refusal to participate in dissection in no way eliminates the rich curiosities needed for geology, anthropology, physics, or even many of the biological sciences pursued at the molecular level. Further, since forcing young students through scientific exercises is one way to turn students off of science, there is a possible counterargument that allowing a choice in dissection matters is far less likely to give science a negative image.

The second type of argument against allowing students the right to make a choice is that the existence of a law permitting students to make this choice harms the business atmosphere. This is an odd argument from one vantage point—in the United States, for example, those states with the most biotechnology research (California and New York) have had dissection choice laws in place for a number of years.

The argument for giving students the right to choose is premised on the notion that dissection choice raises important issues that bear directly on students' moral development. Choice-based legislation in this area clearly gives students the chance to wrestle with a moral issue and thus encourages students to take responsibility for their own choices and actions. The chance to make a choice develops, as it were, children's "ethical muscles." It also encourages respect for a range of competing ideas and their free expression, even as it encourages critical thought regarding the need to take responsibility for one's own actions rather than merely follow the crowd and existing authority.

Thus, for those involved in teaching about the ways in which our society treats, and even sometimes mistreats, the living beings around us, the dissection choice issue offers an important educational opportunity. Some teacher associations have lobbied against the right of children, even with parental consent, to opt out of dissection. In effect, this is an anti-animal rights stance. But it is a narrow-minded approach because it is entirely possible that denying students at this level the chance to make decisions about morally charged matters harms the student's moral development.

What is happening in colleges and universities?

When one finally considers "higher education," the terrain begins to change from that encountered in the earlier levels of formal, classroom-oriented education. Whereas elementary and secondary education is rife with concern for animals, the possibility of living with other animals, and animal protection of many different kinds, education at the level of universities and colleges is a mixed story in two senses. It is "mixed" in that alongside many clubs and student initiatives to help other animals there appear preoccupations that require a dramatic subordination, and even outright dismissal, of nonhuman animal interests.

"Higher education," it turns out, is still dominated by some important cultural assumptions—one of these is that studying subjects outside of science means studying solely human-based matters in a general division of education revealingly named "the humanities." Historically, this was an area of formal education where concerns for "animals" did not fit the prevailing model of maturity. There are still in place many incentives for teachers and administrators at this level to push the worldview that humans are so superior to other animals that humans' use of other animals is not a significant moral issue.

But such a value runs directly against students' natural concerns for other-than-human animals. This is one reason that education at times is set up to favor students who are human-centered, not those who are invested in the larger community of life to which humans clearly belong. Human-centeredness thus remains highly prized and is often touted as a sign of those students whose thinking is not childlike or frivolous.

For this reason, students in higher education exist in an environment where the student clubs can be found along a busy and diverse continuum of student activities. At one end of this continuum are the student clubs focusing on wildlife, ethical food choices and nutrition, companion animals, and ethical treatment of animals. At the other end are "animal science" clubs (more on this below), anti-animal rights groups, and science teachers who insist that adulthood requires leaving sentimentality about "animals" behind.

Universities and colleges in the last 10 years have seen an explosion in courses about animals (such as animals in literature, animals rights, religion and animals, religion and ecology, and many new interdisciplinary and cross-cultural approaches). But these curricular offerings are often single courses, and they must compete with a vast array of established courses where animal issues are not recognized as the kinds of concerns that an "educated" and "cultured" person needs to learn.

Administrations at the college level remain skeptical of "animal courses," although increasingly these kinds of courses are sought by students. This in itself is a factor that is opening minds to "animal rights," because colleges and universities today must compete for the attention of high school seniors. For this reason alone, courses that interest new students, which include animal courses, have an increased chance of being recognized as possible additions to the established curriculum. There are, however, still few formal, degree-granting programs (see the next section for a discussion of animal studies).

One reason for this lack of program-level offerings is that it takes time to develop degree-granting programs, which are almost always found in the long-established disciplines of the humanities and sciences. These degree-granting disciplines are often portrayed as "serious" subjects, whereas new topics are seen as faddish and less substantial. But the emergence of women's studies, minority studies, and cross-cultural studies reveals that the university environment has the capacity to add new, essential subjects. And animal studies programs are thus a serious possibility today.

The emergence of the field "animal science" in universities is an important trend. The general-sounding name can mislead, for while many different sciences have contributed greatly to our understanding of the diversity and complexity of other animals as they live their lives in their communities (see chapter 9 in particular), the term "animal science" is employed quite narrowly. It designates education that is overwhelmingly production-oriented, and it supports existing industrial uses of certain nonhuman animals. The philosopher Bernard Rollin was quoted in chapter 2 regarding one colleague's comment that the morphing of the field "animal husbandry" into the production-oriented field of "animal science" was "the worst thing that ever happened to his department." The discoveries that interest today's researchers in this field are, by and large, "breakthroughs" that allow ever-greater production and efficiency in the use of other-than-human animals as resources for profit-oriented industries. "Breakthroughs" about sentience, or suffering, or cognitive abilities are, not surprisingly, of little interest—in fact, scientists and educators in the animal science field are on the whole rather skeptical about such things.

The result is that questions from students or faculty members that challenge the basic enterprise of using nonhuman animals as mere resources produce tension in the university environment today. This is so because the real priority of animal science is not student learning or freedom to exercise ethical muscles to ask questions about whether it is right to harm sentient, intelligent beings. Questions that suggest the possibility of going back to the ancient husbandry relationship with farm and production animals whereby the animals had to be treated well are often not welcome in such classes. Students often have natural questions about the ways in which the industry-dominated field called "animal science" teaches students to treat other living beings. These questions are welcome in a few courses, but they are often quickly dismissed by animal science faculty as driven by an "animal rights" agenda.

For this reason, many students interested in animal issues find "animal science" to be anathema. Animal science thus represents how strange and new are the modern dismissals of other living beings that prevail in many circles of modern industrialized societies. It is not animal science but another field entirely within universities that today tends to excite students turned off by the industrial mind-set of animal science. We turn next to this new field.

What is the field of "animal studies"?

As mentioned in chapter 4, the new field of animal studies is one of the contributors to telling humans' story with other living beings. Because humans' relationships with the many kinds of beings outside our own species are unfathomably rich and complex, the field of "animal studies" is necessarily more like an umbrella under which one finds a startling variety of diverse approaches. Today, one finds animal studies courses driven by insights from many different disciplines, including history, literature, law, religion, geography, anthropology, sociology, philosophy, and on and on.

These disciplines are classic examples of "the humanities" or social sciences. As such, they have often had humans, not *nonhumans*, as their primary focus. But historians, educators about literature, lawyers, people of religious faith, geographers, anthropologists, sociologists, and many others have long known about the rich relationships humans have had with other animals in many places, eras, and cultures.

Arguably, *any* enterprise that aspires to the name "higher education" must include more than the present dualism of "sciences and humanities" for a number of reasons. Humans' relationships with other living beings need to be understood if our entire set of human abilities is to be engaged by our formal education systems. Similarly, the features of specific ecosystems and their nonhuman citizens must be carefully identified and studied as well, if we wish to understand ourselves in our true context.

For this reason, the dualism of "sciences and humanities" needs to be expanded. A more realistic approach would be a "science, humanities, animals studies" approach. One reason for expanding the present science/humanities dualism is that the humanities are now in fact an unmanageable mega-field composed of a bewildering variety of disciplines held together by human-centeredness. Science is the other mega-field of modern education, and it is home to a rich variety of disciplines that pursue other animals' realities for their own sake. Animal studies can bridge the humanities and the sciences, and also give a central role to environmental/ecological dimensions of life on Earth.

Expanding higher education to include more than the sciences and the humanities is not in any way a repudiation of the importance of these important subjects but a plea to move away from debilitatingly narrow, human-centered approaches to the rich array of topics that exist because of many people's concerns for other-than-human animals. This is, in effect, a kind of "animal rights" approach in that it opens up education to the historic and cultural values of compassion and connection with the more-than-human world. Such fundamental human virtues are shunted aside in higher education today because the science/humanities dualism promotes a myopic approach to nonhuman issues.

The beneficiaries of such a new approach would not be merely nonhuman animals but humans as well. If we are to do "sciences" effectively, our educational curricula need to be complemented not only by the human-centered "humanities" but also by a healthy focus on the more-than-human parts of our shared world. Similarly, if our children are to appreciate the depths of the "humanities" to the fullest, our educational curricula need to be realistic about the *full* context in which our lives play out, namely, the ecologically interwoven world that is our home. Introducing "animal studies" and ecologically sophisticated courses would create interdisciplinary possibilities that go beyond the limitations of the dualistic "arts (humanities) and sciences" mentality that now dominates modern "higher" education.

What is the role of the professions and professional schools?

The emergence of "animal law" in the legal profession, which is discussed in chapter 5, still remains in its first stage or wave, and it will be interesting to see where the second wave takes this interesting field. In other professions, animal protection has been a controversial subject for a longer time. In the medical profession in the early twentieth century, one of the most famous controversies was known as the Brown Dog Affair. This dispute, which lasted from 1903 to 1910, centered on a statue erected in a London suburb to honor a dog that had, solely for educational purposes, been put through multiple medical procedures. In 1907, medical students protesting limits on use of dogs for surgical practice attempted to destroy the statue, which was eventually removed and then later reerected.

Medical research still involves the use of many nonhuman animals, and there are powerful interests that resist calls for changes. But important uses of animals in medical training have long been banned—in the late nineteenth century, for example, the British government radically restricted the use of nonhuman animals for the purpose of surgery practice. Today, more than 90% of medical schools in the United States have followed suit.

Animal protection concerns in the veterinary profession are, to many people's astonishment, also controversial. The modern veterinary profession was started in France in the eighteenth century, and its origins were in military uses of animals. Many individual members of this profession manifested from the very beginning deep concern for the animals themselves, but the profession *as a whole* has been, from the beginning, dominated by utilitarian views of other animals.

From the 1960s onward, however, the veterinary profession and its schools began to develop an important new emphasis on the human-animal bond. This concern amounts to a second heartbeat, as it were, of the profession, for utilitarian uses of animals (originally horses for the military, today food production and medical research based on animal models) remain the primary heartbeat of the profession because they continue to dominate much of veterinary medicine. These two heartbeats can be in tension—for example, while a majority of students entering veterinary school are deeply interested in animal protection, there is a telling absence of "animal rights" clubs in some countries' veterinary schools. In the United States, for example, students applying to veterinary schools are typically afraid to use the words "animal rights" in their application materials, as this would in many instances lower the student's chances of being offered admission to the veterinary school.

Since the 1980s, profession-based groups have emerged to address how each profession has been dealing with other animals. In the United States, for example, profession-related animal study groups exist in at least the following areas since the 1980s.

- American Philosophical Association, Society for the Study of Ethics and Animals (1980)
- NILAS (Nature in Legend and Story) started by faculty members of the Modern Languages Department of Pace University in New York (1989)
- International Society for Anthrozoology (ISAZ) formed in 1991 as a nonprofit organization with worldwide, multidisciplinary membership of students, scholars, and interested professionals.

- American Academy of Religion, Animals and Religion Consultation created informally (1997).
- American Association of Geographers (1998)
- American Sociological Association, Section on Animals and Society (2002).
- American Academy of Religion gives formal status to the Animals and Religion Consultation (2003)
- American Bar Association, Animal Law Committee formally approved (2004)
- American Psychological Association forms the Human-Animals Studies section within the Society of Counseling Psychology (Division 17) (2007)

What has been the role of the arts?

From ancient times, humans' extraordinary abilities with a wide variety of creative arts have been mobilized to engage the relevance and mystery of nonhuman animals for human life. The origins of many important arts, such as dance, painting, and music, are directly connected to human-nonhuman interactions. Dance featured imitation of nonhuman movements and music replication of their sounds (reflected also in the fashioning of musical instruments in the shape of animals). These connections reveal the ancient roots of our interest in other living beings.

Poetry has long celebrated the human-nonhuman interaction. Similarly, animal images of the most diverse kinds appear regularly in religious scriptures, stories, and rituals. One scholar counted references to 113 different kinds of animals in the documents we variously know as the Hebrew Bible or Old Testament. This kind of variety is also typical of the Qur'an, the multiple Hindu and Buddhist scriptures, ancient Chinese texts such as the Tao Te Ching, and indigenous traditions' stories and myths.

Even as creative humans have for millennia created art works reflecting profound interest in other-than-human animals of all kinds, such work has existed alongside the natural preoccupation humans have with our own species. Much in art traditions for obvious reasons reflects the human world, such as the tendencies within western art to focus heavily on human portraiture. But if one looks in the background of even those paintings that give greatest prominence to human figures, quite often there are other animals at the margins.

9

CONTEMPORARY SCIENCES—
NATURAL AND SOCIAL

Just as the major human endeavors of law, education, religion, and various fields like literature and the study of history reveal humans' diverse engagement with other living beings, so too do many sciences reveal that humans and other animals are connected in important ways. In this section, we look at both natural and social sciences. In combination, these important human endeavors create levels of awareness that make it possible for more and more people to recognize the depth and breadth of human-nonhuman possibilities. Further, these sciences provide much information that is relevant to how fields like law, social planning, education, public policy, and even business go forward into the future.

What is the role of science generally in our knowledge and treatment of animals outside our species?

Our many different sciences play a number of key roles with regard to human claims about other animals. Individual sciences have provided confirmation of many commonsense observations about other living beings. Of perhaps even greater significance is that science has at times helped us make corrections, both major and minor, to what initially seem commonsense ideas about other living beings. A third and perhaps most important role played by science is providing detailed information about the actual realities of other living beings.

Science is also a very powerful tradition politically. This power, which is held in government and private institutions, in profit-oriented and nonprofit corporations, and in the education establishment, is a two-edged sword. Science's power stems from the foundational, organizing commitment to the search for truth, providing detailed information about the extraordinary abilities of other animals. In other areas as well, science has "delivered the goods" through its many discoveries that have created business and technological options.

A different kind of power also accrues to the scientific establishment because of its many successes. Government and private funding of science today is extraordinary, and when money is linked to a nonscientific agenda, such as profits or prestige or advancement of special interests, the political clout of science institutions can then retard inquiry that does not promote such motives.

This is important when it comes to inquiries about other animals. Some nonhuman animals have value as mere resources, and the field of animal science is one where instrumental uses of animals as property override their inherent qualities. In chapter 2, the number of pigs slaughtered on just a single day in November 2009 within but a single country (the United States, which after China is the largest slaughterer of pigs) is listed as 433,000. These pigs were owned mostly by large corporations, and they were used to make a variety of consumer food products. The science pursued by these corporations is not in any way concerned with the significance of pigs' evident intelligence, and little science, if any, is today done on these animals' suffering as social beings forced to live in crowded factory farms.

Practicing scientists are disinclined to provide information that might make slaughter of these animals a controversial moral issue. This startles few people familiar with the history of science, for the science establishment has in many instances been done in favor of special interests. The science establishment has protected practices that are harmful to *humans* (such as sale of products like tobacco and asbestos, or the infliction of environmental damage, or the making of public health decisions that favor some human group over another). Not surprisingly, then, there is today much resistance to calls for protection of nonhuman animals in many circles of the scientific establishment because nonhuman animals are so often thought of merely as valuable resources.

The scientific establishment has thus played dual roles: it has helped immensely with discoveries of intelligence, communication, and other remarkable traits in some nonhumans, but it has also been instrumental in helping humans dominate and exploit other animals. Further, along with educational institutions, the science establishment has enabled humans to become effective vandals of the natural habitats of other living beings.

Which natural sciences have played important roles in our understanding of animals?

Charles Darwin's ideas are by far the best-known scientific views about our fellow animals. But historically the role of Aristotle's science must also be taken into account, for Aristotle's body of work stood for more than 1,500 years as the primary source of western cultural thinking about the living beings beyond the human species. Aristotle was a hierarchical thinker when he contemplated nature, and he promoted a famous analogy—as plants are for animals' use, so animals are for humans' use. This analogy is a problem, given that we know humans are animals as fully as are members of any nonhuman species. But Aristotle's faulty analogy remains important in animal rights matters because it is still extremely influential in much of western culture and its institutions as they attempt to justify the privileges that flow from humans' domination over other living beings.

Darwin's insights undermined the prevailing Aristotelian worldview that had advanced hierarchical notions putting humans at the top of all life. His argument took strength from modern science's emphasis on empirical data as a key to assessing the world. It also took strength from its willingness to depart from traditional views that humans were the pinnacle of and reason for creation. Darwin's ideas thus helped minimize the human-centered worldview that members of western cultures inherited with birth and religion.

Darwin's factually detailed argument also helped dispel the notion that each animal species was static, had its own distinctive purpose, and was such that each and every member of the species shared a special "nature" that made the species distinct from all others. In understanding the evolution of ideas about "animals," it is important to know that Darwin's ideas did not win out immediately upon publication, in 1859, of his landmark *On the Origin of Species by Means of Natural Selection*. Seventy years were to pass during which Darwin's general ideas were bandied about by many commentators for many purposes.

Around 1930, a new era in Darwin-influenced thinking began when mathematically trained thinkers linked the idea of Darwinian selection with the nineteenth-century discoveries of the monk Gregor Mendel regarding inheritance (these were the key discoveries that led to the science of genetics). This combination formed the foundations of a synthesis now generally called neo-Darwinism. It is, scientifically speaking, the set of ideas about animals that prevails today. But as many know, in some countries these ideas have politically powerful opponents, a fact which is relevant to the prospects of animal protection proposals that come at a cost to the human community. In many ways, the political world still follows a sense of hierarchy not unlike the notions that Aristotle advanced in the early fourth century B.C.E.

In eastern cultures, there were scientific traditions as well, but these were heavily focused on healing, mathematics, and astronomy. Ideas about animals outside the human species had long been handled in these cultures by religio-ethical traditions. These often featured much knowledge about the natural history of some animals, such as elephants, but there was no real systematization of these ideas into anything like the western scientific tradition's taxonomy of animals.

Today, the general category we call "natural sciences" is dominated by approaches developed in the western scientific tradition. The individual fields in this area have expanded greatly, and the subdivision we know as "the life sciences" includes a bewildering forest of sciences that engage one dimension or another of other living beings' complex of features. The general subject of "biology" is now taught with a heavy emphasis not on whole animals in their communities but on the molecular and cell levels of living organisms, as well as on genetics. The study of whole animals as living members of communities is found in different, more specific life sciences with names like ethology, zoology, ichthyology, entomology, marine mammal science, primatology, and on and on.

Each of these specific life sciences has produced extraordinary information about one set of animals or another. The field of genetics has provided detailed maps that reflect how closely related humans are to many other living beings. Primatology has generated detailed information on the discovery of nonhuman "cultures" among some primate groups. The social complexities of other big-brained social mammals has been pursued in the context of marine mammalogy and elephant studies. The fields known as cognitive science and comparative cognitive ethology have provided interesting and challenging information about not only popular animals like other primates, elephants, whales, dogs, and wolves but also less well-known animals like African gray parrots.

Meanwhile the sciences that fall under the general heading "ecology" or "environmental sciences" have produced profoundly interesting information and perspectives on humans and other animals as members of a world that is vitally interconnected. This is pertinent for a number of reasons. Genetically similar animals often have similar abilities, suggesting that some version of our remarkable human abilities might appear in some of our cousin species. Further, ecological perspectives have also helped us realize that the loss of one species of animal risks much larger problems, like the crash of an entire ecosystem. In addition, system-wide problems like pollution or global climate change are now recognized to threaten all life, not just those species, like polar bears, most evidently in decline from the negative effects of pollution or climate change.

The field of "animal sciences" (discussed in chapters 2 and 8 as the successor to the traditional field "animal husbandry") is an unusual science, for, as already pointed out, research in this field is not broad in the way that inquiries in ethology or cognitive sciences are open-minded. The latter are wonderful examples of investigative science where researchers and students are looking generally and willing to report anything they find to be of scientific interest. Research in "animal science" is characteristically within a narrow range intended solely to extend existing efficiencies, not to produce new knowledge that might lead an ethics-sensitive student or researcher to challenge the right of businesses to make a profit from use of the animals.

Which social sciences today contribute to our understanding of animals?

Given that humans are social animals, application of social science survey methods to human communities has produced uniquely important information on the extent and nature of human/nonhuman relationships in the contemporary world. Not only are companion animals treasured, but a very high percentage of citizens in industrialized countries—as high as 99% in some polls—identify their companion animals as *family* members. Sociological analyses produce important perspectives on the range and depth of interactions with dogs, cats, birds, exotic pets, feral animals, and wildlife within communities and in conservation areas. Sociology has also produced important studies on the interrelation of violence against nonhuman animals and violence against humans.

The impressive field of geography has pioneered many different approaches by which we can look at the interactions of humans with local nonhumans. Today the range of studies is great, and it includes not only studies of humans' interactions with nonhumans around the globe but also urban-based studies of the kind mentioned in chapter 7.

Anthropology has long been a leading source of information about cultural variety among humans. Since political scientists, economists, sociologists, and other social scientists dominated study of "the civilized world," anthropology in the nineteenth century pioneered the study of indigenous peoples. It often did this during its first decades with a bias for western society as the highest form of civilization. But in more recent years anthropologists have become a rich source for helpful perspectives on the astounding variety of human cultures as they have reacted in their idiosyncratic ways to local fauna.

One of the most powerful and yet controversial social sciences today is the field of economics. Referred to as "the dismal science" by Thomas Carlyle, this important social science has a heavy preoccupation with humans and, in particular, human consumers. It has long been influential in public policy decisions, and more recently it has gained much influence in the important "law and economics" discussion by which future laws are assessed on the grounds of economics-driven assumptions. What is important for animal issues is that economists are valuable allies, because some animal-friendly enterprises are thriving today (an example is given in chapter 6).

The fields of sociology, geography, anthropology, and economics hardly exhaust the many ways social sciences can illuminate what humans have been doing and are now doing regarding "animals." Other social sciences already mentioned—education, law, and political science—have historically been dominated by human-centered perspectives. But as suggested above, these fields can, if opened up, easily become part of a productive dialogue about the inevitable interaction that humans have with the many forms of nonhuman life sharing the world with us.

Which animals are intelligent or self-aware?

Many people easily notice that a variety of other animals seem to have various kinds of intelligence. For centuries, many in western cultures assumed human intelligence was the measure of all intelligence; in fact, some humans claimed that humans' capacity to reason was just like that of the divinity who created the world. In this worldview, other beings' intelligence was a pale reflection of what humans had in full measure.

But there are strong reasons to suspect that human intelligence is not the measure of all intelligence. One reason was suggested in the early 1980s by the psychologist Howard Gardner, who observed that humans have "multiple intelligences." Originally Gardner suggested seven different kinds of intelligence—linguistic, logical-mathematical, spatial, musical, bodily-kinesthetic, interpersonal, and intrapersonal. In 1997 Gardner added "naturalistic" intelligence as an eighth form of intelligence that humans reflect. Human wisdom traditions have long observed that human intelligence is far more than mere logic, and it surely goes beyond the vague notion of "reason," however one defines it. Given that common sense suggests that other animals have some form of intelligence, it is worth exploring whether they too have multiple kinds of intelligence, some of which may or may not be shared by humans.

It is possible, for example, that some nonhumans, especially those closely related to humans, may share some of the different kinds of intelligence which humans have. Also, given that many animals have brains structured exactly as human brains are structured, and given that some other animals have larger brains than humans do (sperm whales have the largest), there is further reason to be open-minded about intelligence in some other animals.

Even more intriguing, since other animals often have sensory abilities that humans do not have, it makes sense that other animals could have intelligence(s) of a kind different from those that humans have. We can ask, for example, what do dolphins do with the highly sophisticated echolocation abilities? We can also be honest enough to admit that our intelligences may be just some of the forms of awareness and inquiry that are possible.

One deeply interesting and familiar form of awareness is self-awareness. This is hard to measure, but a number of non-human animals have passed special tests originally designed for the specific purpose of confirming humans' self-awareness. These tests were developed in the late 1960s through the 1970s, and versions of them now have been passed by chimpanzees, bonobos, at least one gorilla, orangutans, and bottlenose dolphins.

Other animals, including elephants, also display what appear to be features of self-awareness. These animals are obviously intelligent in a variety of ways, but some do not pass the classic tests devised for *human* self-awareness. These tests may be biased because they are based on sight, which is humans' dominant sensory ability. Because we are bright enough to notice this problem, we can wonder if other tests not yet devised might confirm that nose-oriented animals, like elephants or dogs, easily pass self-awareness tests based on smell. In other words, there may well be different kinds or levels of self-awareness, and we now recognize that our formulation of this issue needs to remain flexible.

That some nonhumans could qualify for our moral concern even though they have a different kind or level of awareness than we do is an important humility on our part. Recognition of this possibility depends on significant contributions by people from different human fields, such as cognitive science, philosophy, and ethics. Communication studies show that many living beings communicate in a startling variety of ways, some of which occur in unexpected animals, like the bird Alex mentioned in chapters 2 and 6.

Do other animals have their own communities?

That other animals live in communities is an ancient idea. Chapter 6 quotes a passage from the Qur'an suggesting community: "There is not a thing that moves on the earth, no bird that flies on its wings, but has a community of its own like yours." The realities of other animals' communities are being confirmed in countless ways by modern sciences, including the powerful science of ethology, which carries a variety of tools for looking at other animals' behavior in context. In addition, the newly emerged field of "animal personality" has been enriched since the early 1990s by a growing number of researchers from a broad range of disciplines, including psychology, evolutionary biology and ecology, and animal behavior. In 1993, the *Journal of Comparative Psychology* published an article titled "Personalities of Octopuses" as the first-ever documentation of personality in invertebrates. Since then, the term "personality" has regularly been applied in scientific publications to a wide range of nonhuman animals, including a variety of primates, hyenas, different birds, stickleback fish, and giant octopuses.

Do animals have emotions?

Emotions in other animals, which many other cultures have long assumed to exist, have been alluded to in a variety of chapters—many people today are confident that they recognize emotions in other animals, despite denials by a few scientists and philosophers that such emotions exist.

Early twentieth-century science in the western cultural tradition confidently dismissed this possibility. But in the 1960s, modern science underwent yet another revolution when cognitive scientists like Donald Griffin of Harvard University pioneered a return to common sense on issues like consciousness, self-awareness, and emotions in other living beings. Today, many scientists work on this extraordinary issue. Marc Bekoff's 2007 book *The Emotional Lives of Animals* carries the subtitle "A Leading Scientist Explores Animal Joy, Sorrow, and Empathy, and Why They Matter." Bekoff's argument is steeped in science as he points out that today's scientific debates focus on why animal emotions have evolved the way they have, *not whether they exist*. Bekoff invokes a scientific criterion when he confidently asserts, "It's bad biology to argue against the existence of animal emotions." Bekoff then backs up this commonsense claim with information about various nonhumans' abilities to care.

The practical, animal rights dimension of this is made evident in a comment by the founder of the Elephant Sanctuary in Tennessee. Whenever she is asked about the emotions of elephants, Carol Buckley (see chapter 10) responds directly, "I consider elephants a walking body of emotion. Their lives revolve around relationships which are continually deepening."

10

MAJOR FIGURES AND ORGANIZATIONS IN THE ANIMAL RIGHTS MOVEMENT

The individuals and organizations listed here are mentioned because they have made a difference somewhere and thus become revealing parts of the worldwide animal protection movement. Some are very well known, even famous. Peter Singer is, for example, a high-profile philosopher at Princeton University in the United States and sometimes described as "the best known philosopher in the world." Albert Schweitzer is for some a household name, and others will surely recognize Ingrid Newkirk and her organization, People for the Ethical Treatment of Animals.

But most of the other individuals and organizations described below will be unfamiliar names, even though they have made a significant contribution locally, nationally, or even internationally. Some of the individuals work for high-profile organizations, but it is their work as individuals that led to their inclusion in this list. The people on this list in different ways model how individuals, including those "behind the scenes," play essential parts in putting together the complex puzzle that forms today's animal rights movement as it seeks fundamental, effective protections for nonhuman animals of one kind or another.

Two Pioneers—Salt and Spira

Henry Salt lived from 1851 to 1939. An English citizen who campaigned actively for many kinds of social reform, Salt exemplified a feature characteristic of many, though not all, animal rights advocates—he worked extremely hard on *human* issues as well. He cared immensely about prison reform and education reform, challenged economic institutions to be more responsive to a wider range of people, and campaigned against the flogging of sailors. His contribution to the animal rights movement was immense, for in 1892 he published *Animals' Rights Considered in Relation to Social Progress.* The prefatory note of this book stated succinctly, "The object of the following essay is to set the principle of animals' rights on a consistent and intelligible footing, to show that this principle underlies the various efforts of humanitarian reformers." Salt's commitments led him in 1891 to found the Humanitarian League, a group concerned with the suffering of any sentient being.

For Salt, as for so many others in this section, campaigning against harms to other animals was part of a tradition of dissent that worked toward emancipation of marginalized human groups. Although reformers typically spoke of "animals" or "brute creation" as separate from humans, implicitly these reformers recognized the connection of these other beings to humans—both suffer from pain and injustice, which made animal protection of a piece with the deep feelings that also inspired campaigns against slavery, mistreatment of prisoners, and the radical subordination of women.

Henry Spira was a pioneer of a different kind. Like Salt, his activism was grounded in work on behalf of disadvantaged humans, through labor organizing. Spira created change on a variety of animal issues without the benefit of money or an organization. In 1975, after learning about experiments on cats being conducted at New York's Museum of Natural History, Spira attempted to open a dialogue with the researcher and the administrators of the institution regarding the experiments (Spira had acquired his first cat in 1973). When he received no response, Spira turned to local media, then public demonstrations and full-page ads in the *New York Times*. In 1977, the museum agreed to stop the experiments because Spira's campaign had generated much popular support. After this success, Spira then embarked on successful campaigns that led to Amnesty International repudiating any use of live animals in experiments and, most important of all, to major cosmetic companies, including Revlon and Avon, agreeing to refrain from harmful testing of cosmetics on animals. This latter campaign led to the cruelty-free labeling on many of today's cosmetics products.

Two Theologians—Schweitzer and Linzey

Albert Schweitzer's name is synonymous with reverence for life. A world-famous doctor and an accomplished historian, musician, and scholar of religion, Schweitzer, who lived from 1875 to 1965, worked tirelessly for both humans and nonhumans. Today he is deeply respected all over the world. He models an interdisciplinary approach to caring about all life.

Andrew Linzey (1952–present) comes from a domain that some consider the most unlikely of places to find an advocate for nonhuman animals—the world of academic theology. Linzey's creative work has made him by far the best-known modern advocate of "animal theology," which Linzey suggests leads any believer to recognize a God-given duty to protect life. Linzey has taught at Oxford University since the 1990s and continues to publish and lecture widely.

Schweitzer and Linzey exemplify decades of work within one religion (Christianity) that has often been described as at best unresponsive to nonhumans, at worst the cause of the complete dismissal of nonhuman animals in western societies (the last idea is a famous thesis by the historian Lynn White Jr.). Their lives together reveal that religious traditions can be a rich source of animal rights creativity.

Insightful Woman Pioneers—Ruth Harrison and Rosalind Godlovitch

These two women pioneered new ideas about animal protection in England in the 1960s. In doing so, they inspired many others, including the young Peter Singer when he was at Oxford University. Today these names are not known in the way Schweitzer's and Singer's names are recognized, but these women represent well the fact that the animal protection movement of modern times has been built up by countless people of insight and deep commitment over decades. In particular, they represent the seminal role that women have played from the very beginning of the modern animal rights movement. Today, a large majority of members and volunteers in animal rights organizations are women.

Ruth Harrison in 1964 published *Animal Machines: The New Factory Farming Industry*, the first detailed analysis of modern production methods that treated food animals as mere commodities to be handled solely under the logic of industrial science rather than the ancient husbandry values that had been built up by our ancestors. The book is out of print today, but it was historically important because it started the tradition of frank descriptions of a process that to this day remains hidden from view behind security gates.

A decade later in 1973, Rosalind Godlovitch was one of three editors of a collection of essays called *Animals, Men and Morals: An Enquiry into the Maltreatment of Non-humans*. This book broke ground by including a range of essays that call out the questionable arguments often used to support traditional practices, and in this Godlovitch's work is the forerunner of the scores of essay collections that address one or more animal-related problems around the modern world.

Key Philosophers—Peter Singer and Tom Regan

These two are the animal rights movement's best-known philosophers. Singer, an Australian who is a tenured professor at Princeton University, was described, in 2000 in the *New York Times Book Review* as "the most influential living philosopher." Singer's best-selling 1975 book *Animal Liberation: A New Ethic for Our Treatment of Animals*, which has often been described as "the Bible of the animal rights movement," provided many details about the use of research and food animals. Singer urged his readers to conclude that many current practices harming other animals constituted, upon close examination, unethical behavior. Singer's many influential essays and books, such as *Practical Ethics*, argue in the tradition of utilitarianism that humans should employ a principle of "equal consideration of interests" in assessing whether actions harming nonhuman animals can be justified in any way. Singer's work has drawn an astonishing amount of attention, and he has also been called "the most dangerous man in the world" by religious conservatives angered by his criticism of Christianity on animal issues and his views on euthanasia of humans.

Tom Regan is an American philosopher whose 1984 book, *The Case for Animal Rights*, is often described as the most developed philosophical argument for animal rights. Regan argues for moral rights for those nonhuman animals that he defines as "subjects of a life." In his philosophical argument, Regan models how detailed critical thinking can be brought to bear on the ethical dimensions of humans' encounter with other living beings. Regan has modeled much else in his long, productive life. He has supported many other thinkers about animal issues and has been instrumental in establishing North Carolina State University's important historical archive for the animal rights movement and the Culture and Animals Foundation.

Regan is the best known of the rights-based philosophers (see chapter 3), while Singer is the best-known utilitarian philosopher.

That these very different kinds of philosophers are both leaders in the animal protection movement reveals that from its inception, the modern animal rights movement was grounded in a variety of views about the importance of some beings beyond the species line.

From Welfare to Rights—Richard Ryder and Bernard Rollin

Richard Ryder and Bernard Rollin have made huge differences in their respective countries (Britain and the United States). Each is a rights-oriented thinker who led efforts on welfare-focused legislation in his own country (Rollin has also worked on Canadian issues). Such legislation has made possible further steps toward *rights*-based legislation, and thus demonstrates that the rights-welfare distinction is by no means absolute.

Ryder has long worked with the Royal Society for the Prevention of Cruelty to Animals, and coined the term "speciesism" in 1970. He continues to work with cabinet-level administrators in the United Kingdom. Rollin, a distinguished professor at Colorado State University with an appointment in philosophy and veterinary medicine, is arguably the world's leading veterinary ethicist. He has worked on major federal legislation and published dozens of books and articles on ethics, pain, farm animal welfare, the history of science, and much more.

Creative Pioneering across Boundaries—Betty Lawrence and Carol Adams

Elizabeth "Betty" Atwood Lawrence (1929–2003) pioneered a scholarly, interdisciplinary approach to animal studies, even as she practiced as a veterinarian and raised a family in a happy marriage. She published five respected books, wrote numerous articles for prestigious journals and collections of edited essays, and gave lectures and received awards around the world on a wide variety of animal-related topics. She shows how someone who cares about nonhuman animals can live a full, family-oriented life and still make a major contribution.

Carol Adams is a feminist and theorist who has pushed the women's movement, animal advocates, and educators to engage other animals as a topic with personal, political, ethical, and educational importance of the first rank. Her many books, the best known of which is *The Sexual Politics of Meat: A Feminist-Vegetarian Critical Theory* (1991), raise a rich array of issues in uniquely creative ways. Adams demonstrates how individuals can participate fully in different liberation movements at the same time.

The Law Arrives—Joyce Tischler and Steven Wise

These two American lawyers have made a difference in the course of more than three decades of work. Tischler founded the Animal Legal Defense Fund (ALDF) in 1979 and has developed it into the world's most successful law-based group addressing animal issues in a range of countries. Tischler and ALDF have not only led sustained efforts in litigation (especially regarding companion animal and cruelty issues) but have also promoted protective legislation of many kinds. Of particular practical importance is the assistance that Tischler's nonprofit group has given to local prosecutors and private attorneys as they work on animal-related problems in countless jurisdictions. ALDF has also been instrumental in the important area of drafting wills and trusts that protect animals after their owner's death. ALDF is also the principal force behind student-led efforts to secure animal law courses in law schools around the world. In these and virtually countless other ways, Tischler has modeled how an individual can grow an organization that provides practical advice, even as it expands the litigation, legislative and education frontiers of animal law.

Steven M. Wise is also a pioneer in animal law. He has long championed use of legal research methods and academic papers to develop the idea that specific legal rights should be granted to some nonhuman animals. In 2002, Wise published the groundbreaking *Rattling the Cage: Toward Legal Rights for Animals*, which argues that the core values in common law legal systems support the conclusion that bonobos and chimpanzees should be given specific legal rights. This book was the first systematic argument about why legal rights make sense in terms of a legal system's own values. Wise continues to expand the legal community's notion of what is possible in animal law through publication of research papers and books.

From New Zealand to Austria—Barbara Leonard and Martin Balluch

These individuals are two ordinary citizens among others. Barbara Leonard and Martin Balluch are included because they made a difference by advancing major animal rights legislation in, respectively, New Zealand and Austria. In their success on opposite sides of the world, they are not at all ordinary; instead, they model well the truth in this oft-quoted comment by Margaret Mead: "Never doubt that a small group of committed citizens can change the world. Indeed, it is the only thing that ever has."

Barbara Leonard was instrumental in the September 1999 passage of legislation in New Zealand known as the Animal Welfare Act. The principal sponsor of the legislation was The Great Ape Project–New Zealand, of which Leonard was an integral part. While the enacted protections were considerably narrower than the original legislative proposal, and the new law does not use the word "rights" in any way, this law provided dramatically new protections that were reported around the world as a stunning animal rights success. The bill was not postured internally within New Zealand as an animal rights measure, and it did not seek the liberty of the nonhuman great apes covered by this newly enacted legislation. But the new legislation was cutting edge in banning "hominid" experimentation that could not be shown to be in the interest of the individual or in the interest of the species to which the individual belongs and not unduly harmful to the individual. Leonard and her group model well how a small group of local citizens in a country can prompt fundamental, law-based protections in the tradition of moral animal rights, even though these protections are not themselves couched in the language of specific legal rights.

Martin Balluch was similarly instrumental in the 2005 decision of both chambers of the Austrian parliament to ban ape experiments unless they are shown to be in the interest of the experimental subject. This legislation models how individual countries go forward on policy decisions about other animals. No experiments on apes had been conducted in Austria since 2002, but as Balluch said, "This decision will send a signal to the rest of Europe and the world, where such experiments still take place: civilized countries consider it unacceptable to allow any kind of experiments on apes. That should have a ripple-on effect to stop such experiments elsewhere, like the fur farm ban in Austria eventually helped to trigger a similar ban for example in England."

Sanctuary—Carole Noon, Dame Sheldrick, Carol Buckley, Lisa Kane

These four women have led sanctuary and rescue efforts of singular success. Dr. Carole Noon (1949–2009), a biological anthropologist who founded the rescue and sanctuary organization Save the Chimps, led the effort to establish the world's largest sanctuary for captive chimpanzees at the Center for Captive Chimpanzee Care in Florida. She raised extraordinary amounts of money, lobbied effectively to free hundreds of chimpanzees from biomedical researchers, and then provided not only effective sanctuary but an ongoing organization that continues to provide a retirement home for chimpanzees rescued from biomedical research, entertainment, and private owners. When asked the common question about why she allocated so much effort to caring for chimpanzees when children were going hungry, Noon was known to reply, "I'm always taken aback by the question because I don't view the world in two halves—eating chimps and starving children. Except for a few percent of DNA, they're us." Noon shows the difference an individual can make in the lives of many animals that have been given up for lost.

Dame Daphne Sheldrick is well known for her innovative successes with orphan elephants in Kenya. The ivory trade has led to the killing of many elephants, and in Kenya alone the population had been reduced from well over 100,000 elephants in the 1980s to as few as 16,000. The result is an astonishing number of orphan elephants. In 1986, Kenyan-born Sheldrick helped develop a dietary formula for elephant infants. After obtaining government permission to establish an orphanage, she successfully pioneered methods for raising them and then, when the young elephants are old enough, reintroducing them to the wild. Sheldrick has been widely recognized for this work, in which keepers spend many hours with the young elephants to, as Sheldrick says, "replace what the elephant would have had in the wild with its natural family."

Carol Buckley is an American who in 1995 founded a different kind of sanctuary—a natural-habitat refuge for sick, old, and needy Asian elephants. Located in Tennessee, the Elephant Sanctuary was founded by Buckley because of her concern for Tarra, a female Asian elephant born in Burma. Tarra spent more than a year living in the back of a delivery truck, then in a store's parking lot during the day and a residential driveway at night. Buckley took responsibility for Tarra's welfare, and the result was the Elephant Sanctuary. The refuge now includes African elephants, although this different species is housed separately from the resident Asian elephants.

Buckley's experience taught her, "They are all individuals, so their reaction to captivity has taken different forms. For most zoo elephants the amount of physical freedom is daunting. For circus elephants, they have a hard time trusting that they will not be controlled or punished. What they all seem to have in common is the disbelief that their caregivers are so attentive to their needs." When asked what she has learned from working with elephants, Buckley is known to answer with a single word: "Compassion." In this regard, Buckley echoes comments made by Sheldrick in the book *An Elephant in the Room: The Science and Well-being of Elephants in Captivity:*

> Elephants are emotionally very "human" animals, sharing with us the same emotions that govern our own lives, plus an identical age progression, the same sense of family, sense of death, loves and loyalties that span a lifetime, and many other very 'human' traits, including compassion. They have also been endowed with other attributes we humans do not possess, such as innate knowledge in a genetic memory.... [I]n such a long-lived species, there is also a lifetime of learning through experience, just as there is for humans.

Lisa Kane is an American activist who has worked on behalf of captive elephants for decades. She models how someone who has a full-time job can nonetheless lead a group of activists around the world as they address a fundamental problem. Kane was one of the leaders of the Coalition for Captive Elephant Well-Being. She is the lead author of *Optimal Conditions for Captive Elephants* (2005) and *Best Practices for Captive Elephant Well-Being* (2005). These two documents, which propose fundamental revisions in guidelines for handling of captive elephants, were the principal focus of a conference hosted by Tufts University's Cummings School of Veterinary Medicine's Center for Animals and Public Policy. Contributors to this conference, which is described in *An Elephant in the Room,* included elephant experts and zoo representatives from Europe, Asia, Africa, Australia, and the United States.

Leadership in India—Maneka Gandhi and Raj Panjwani

These are two of the best-known animal rights advocates in India. While they share the role of coauthors of the book *Animal Laws in India*, each performs many other roles involving animal rights.

Maneka Gandhi has held public office in India's Lok Sabha and been a minister in many different Indian governments, including Minister of the Environment and Forests, Minister of State for Social Justice and Empowerment, and Minister for Culture. She also created the Department for Animal Welfare and served as its minister. She is a vegan and has written books for children and a variety of books about animals, including *First Aid for Animals*. In the 1970s, Maneka Gandhi was a widely read columnist writing on animal welfare and environment. She has since created and presented television programs on animals and environment, including the program *Heads and Tails*, which focused on harms and suffering experienced by nonhuman animals due to their commercial exploitation. In 1992, she founded People for Animals, which runs shelters throughout India and is that nation's largest and most visible organization for animal rights. She has been chair of the Delhi Society for Prevention of Cruelty to Animals and the managing trustee of an animal care shelter and hospital. As chair in 1995 of the Committee for the Purpose of Control and Supervision of Experiments on Animals, she directed unannounced inspections of laboratories where animals were used for scientific research.

Raj Panjwani, principal author of the authoritative *Animal Laws of India*, is a leading constitutional law lawyer in India who has been integral to advancing the field of animal law. He has served on many government committees, including the committee appointed by the high court of Delhi for the implementation of laws pertaining to wildlife, the Committee on the Delhi Slaughter House, and the Committee on Stray Animals in Urban Areas. Panjwani is the founder of the Animal and Environment Legal Defense Fund. He has drafted many different pieces of legislation for the government of India, including laws on performing animals, prevention of cruelty, and transport. His law practice has focused on animal welfare, environmental issues and legislation. His successes as an advocate for animal rights include protection of turtles, prohibition on ivory trade, prohibition of trade in furs and skins of endangered animals, improved conditions for animals in circuses and mobile zoos, establishment of procedures for veterinary care of injured or rescued animals, and prohibitions regarding slaughter of stray dogs.

Leadership in China—Song Wei and Jill Robinson

As one of the world's oldest civilizations, China has traditions of care and concern for nonhuman animals that are impressive. But developments in the twentieth century, and in particular the Communist revolution at the midpoint of the century, caused much Chinese tradition to be challenged and ignored. Today China is again a world leader, with hundreds of millions of Chinese having moved out of poverty into a consumer-oriented society. China is now among the world's leading exporters of goods, but this has come at the heavy price of habitat destruction and some of the worst pollution on the planet.

Animal advocacy virtually disappeared in twentieth-century China because it was shorn of its traditional roots, and also disfavored in the postrevolutionary environment. Today there is an emerging animal protection movement, and Song Wei and Jill Robinson are among those at the forefront.

Attorney Song Wei, who is also a professor at the Law of Science and Technology Institute at China's University of Science and Technology, has brought attention to many specific incidents in China where animals were harmed in one way or another. Professor Song in 2000 became the first person to teach the subject animal welfare law in a Chinese university, and he continues today. In 2001 he published the first book about animal welfare legislation in China (*Kind to Animals*). In his writing and speaking, Professor Song strikes a balance between honest description of actual problems today and recognition of China's heritage of animal-friendly perspectives. He continues to speak out and to attend international conferences on animal law issues, and he advocates that China's heritage of wisdom about the importance of taking nonhuman animals seriously be incorporated into modern Chinese animal laws. This tradition has deep roots because it was developed over millennia—it is found not only in Confucius but in sages before and after his time. The tradition continues into the early twentieth century with contributions from writers such as Lu Xun.

Jill Robinson is the founder and leader of the Animals Asia Foundation, which has brought attention to many issues, but she is best known for tireless work since 1993 within China on the problem of bear bile farming. Her approach has been to build relationships that further her negotiations with government agencies that can help end this astonishingly cruel tradition. Her skills produced the first accord between the Chinese government and an outside animal welfare organization, which was a signed pledge in 2000 by which two state agencies agreed to free 500 bears in the province of Sichuan, as well as to work toward elimination of bear farming entirely. Robinson's work in China and other parts of Asia models well how an outsider can respect cultural and political traditions and still be deeply effective.

A singular commitment, a controversial organization—Ingrid Newkirk

Reviled by many, idolized by many, Ingrid Newkirk cofounded and now directs the People for the Ethical Treatment of Animals, or PETA, which has an annual budget in the range of $30 million and is called "the world's largest animal rights organization" by the *Encyclopedia Brittanica*. Born in Britain in 1949, Newkirk is a constant media presence known for controversial observations and advertising campaigns that question any number of practices. Newkirk has led an astonishing number of successful PETA campaigns involving researchers' and industries' use of nonhuman animals. Her work in the undercover investigation of the Silver Spring monkey research led to the first police raid on an animal-research facility in the United States and the first conviction (although subsequently overturned) of an animal researcher, which in turn led to centrally important protections for laboratory animals being added by way of a 1985 amendment to the Animal Welfare Act. Newkirk models as well as anyone does the role that an individual can have in changing practices involving nonhuman animals.

Organizations Together—Wayne Pacelle and Gene Baur

Wayne Pacelle has been the president of the Humane Society of the United States since 2004. Gene Baur is the founder and president of Farm Sanctuary, the first animal rescue organization dedicated to farmed animals. Each of these corporate efforts has had great success. But it is the work of these two organizations together that brings the issue back to the ordinary individual. Pacelle and Baur have led efforts to use voter-based initiatives to address farm animal practices. With an initial success in Florida in 2002 to ban gestation crates for pigs (the popular vote was 55% in favor), followed by a second success in Arizona in 2006 banning gestation crates for pigs and veal crates for male calves (which passed with 62% of the vote), Pacelle and Baur worked together in the most populous American state (California) in 2008 to ban gestation crates, veal crates, and battery cages. As mentioned in chapter 5, this ballot initiative passed with 63% of the vote.

While each of these organization leaders has also been involved in countless legislative efforts on other topics as well, the joint effort of the organizations run by Pacelle and Baur has given the general public a means by which to voice its opinion.

Taking issues to voters has only rarely been the first option and is typically resorted to when other legislative machinery does not work. But in a very special way, such ballot-based initiatives reflect that public policy on animal issues belongs to everyone in the society, and not merely to those who own other living beings as private property.

11

THE FUTURE
OF ANIMAL RIGHTS

In the 1957 documentary *The Battle of Algiers*, directed by Gillo Pontecorvo, the Algerian strategist Larbi Ben M'Hidi says to one activist, "It's hard enough to start a revolution, even harder still to sustain it, and hardest of all to win it. But it is only afterwards, once we've won, that the real difficulties begin."

Today's animal rights movement is multifaceted, in ferment, and thus in motion and flexible. What the world would look like if "animal rights" becomes a deep commitment of the human community depends upon many different factors. This is because protections for other living beings can come in so many different forms. Which forms will be chosen is not always easy to predict. Further, in many ways the future of the animal protection movement already belongs to a new generation as today's youth embrace animal issues, for many young people are already at work expanding the protections that came about because of resurgence in animal rights in the 1970s.

In the future, as discussed in chapter 5, legal rights may become a dominant tool employed on behalf of this or that group of nonhuman animals. But there are many other options as well. These include additional major tools available in the diverse tool box that we know as modern legal systems, which can create effective, fundamental, specific legal protections for specific animals. There are also *many non-law tools* that active citizens working toward animal protection have long utilized. For this reason, the future is likely to see many different forms of protections for other living beings.

Who are the others joining us in the more-than-human community?

The specific animals now being honored by the early twenty-first-century animal rights movement are rather diverse. To determine why we now protect these animals and which others might be included within the circle of protection, we can ask, *why do we protect other living beings at all?*

Any answer to this fundamental question will surely involve a combination of factors, but at the top of the list must be *their realities*, that is, other-than-human animals' actual, day-to-day realities as living beings in their own communities.

Also high on the list will be *our* abilities as ethical creatures to care about a wide range of "others." Our imaginations, open-mindedness, commitments to justice, and compassion will appear on the list as well. For some, an element of self-interest must be included—the factors of relationship, aesthetics (beauty), even following divine commands might suffice to meet one's self-interest. Another self-interested reason for protecting the community of life is that doing so affirms the importance of the human species as well—other animals' realities will not likely be honored in a world where we continue to ignore the realities of other humans whom societies have all too often ignored.

Today we find myriad ways to honor greatly our own companion animals because of who and what they are and what they do for us. As we do this, it must be remembered that members of the very species now treasured are still killed in high numbers in those very societies that are most infatuated with dogs and cats.

We honor greatly whales and dolphins, the nonhuman great apes, elephants, and many other endangered mammals, birds, and reptiles for a variety of reasons. They are important in and of themselves, and yet they enhance our lives and world. But even as some societies move to protect these animals, others use them in experiments or entertainment.

It is true that in some very significant ways we have started to honor even unpopular, nonmammalian species at risk of extinction, and even whole ecosystems. Collectively, however, our species still remains remarkably apathetic about harms to wild populations of some of the most popular animals—it is not only populations of many obscure animals that are at risk. Many species of whales and dolphins, all the nonhuman great apes, and the several species of elephants teeter on the brink of extinction in certain areas. Reports suggest that one in four bird species is now functionally extinct, and one-fourth of the world's mammals are threatened. Even worse numbers appear for "lesser" creatures—the World Conservation Union in 2004 reported that one-third of the amphibians, and more than 40% of all turtles and tortoises are threatened with extinction. In June 2003, it was reported that large, oceanic fish had declined by 90% in the last 50 years.

Closer to home, our cousin primates are in deep trouble—half of primate species are listed as threatened. Closest to home, it was reported as long ago as 2001 that populations of our closest cousins—chimpanzees, bonobos, gorillas, and orang-utans—had declined 93% in the twentieth century. Our record in the first decade of the twenty-first century has not improved much, if at all.

Yet this book documents that human-nonhuman relationships are changing in some encouraging ways as well. The deep ferment has helped us engage our ability to use law, education, voting, and much else to engage some nonhumans. But animal protection issues will continue to develop, no doubt, for we only now begin to consider a wide range of new problems, such as the species impacted by global climate change.

We also have begun to care far more deeply about food animals. Further, we deepen our concern for research animals, even as many in our human community continue to insist adamantly that harming living beings for "science" and our own profit does not raise moral problems.

It would be hard, in the face of so many problems for which we are totally responsible, to disagree that we are complicated animals. The deep and wide—and now diverse—tradition we know as "animal rights" pushes us hard today to reconsider how we act toward other living beings. We have developed a contentious dialogue about the importance, some would say necessity, of using even our most precious resources—legal rights, education time with our children, and religious concern—in the task of finding a way to live with other animals in the more-than-human world we share with them.

So which animals should we protect? Surely the answer is *more than just ourselves.* Yet, as chapter 2 makes clear, the community of life is very busy, dominated by micro animals far more than by macro animals like ourselves. Which living beings from which of the tens of millions of species can we protect? At the end of *On the Origin of Species by Means of Natural Selection,* Darwin used the image of a tangled riverbank.

> It is interesting to contemplate an entangled bank, clothed with many plants of many kinds, with birds singing on the bushes, with various insects flitting about, and with worms crawling through the damp earth, and to reflect that these elaborately constructed forms, so different from each other, and dependent on each other in so complex a manner, have all been produced by laws acting around us.

Darwin ended this final paragraph by marveling at how the earth's simple creatures developed into ever more complicated animals.

> ...the production of the higher animals, directly follows. There is grandeur in this view of life, with its several

powers, having been originally breathed into a few forms or into one; and that, whilst this planet has gone cycling on according to the fixed law of gravity, from so simple a beginning endless forms most beautiful and most wonderful have been, and are being, evolved.

Among these "higher animals" we find virtually all of the beings that today's animal rights movement has noticed and takes seriously. These are typically what have been here called "macro animals," that is, the ones that each of us, as individuals walking out into the world, can notice.

As we notice them, we can sense that these more complicated animals are somewhat like us. And since we know from our own experiences how sentient and intelligent and relationship-bound each of us can be, we now consider protecting some of these macro animals as individuals and as members of their own communities. This is one of the reasons we explain our attention to these nonhuman members of the world community in very elegant terms. We talk today of justice, of noticing their realities, of dogs and cats and horses as family members, of the cultures and communities of chimpanzees or dolphins or elephants, of the brains of sperm whales, of the emotions of elephants and dogs, and on and on.

Above all, though, we talk of compassion, for other than hunting and being hunted by them, this is our longest standing human tradition about other animals. It is clear that our compassion is enhanced when we are familiar with other animals, when we notice their realities, for then we can mobilize our remarkable ethical abilities and thereby take these animal individuals seriously. To do this, we must at times use our remarkable imaginations, for it is this skill that helps us get across the species line.

It is these special human abilities—ethics and imagination—that open us up to learning of all kinds. And without question, given these abilities and the fascinating realities of other animals, we will learn much in the coming decades.

Can ethics work hand in hand with science?

The answer to this fundamental question is yes, without question. There are those who are hesitant about this—many in the science establishment are suspicious of "ethics" as "mere opinion," just as they are concerned about any talk that hints at spirituality. So, not surprisingly in circles where other animals are used, Upton Sinclair's observation that it is "difficult to get a man to understand something when his salary depends upon his not understanding it" yet again helps us understand why certain opinions prevail.

Some circles of veterinary medicine (see chapters 2 and 8) ironically manifest extreme discomfort with animal rights in general and more particularly with claims that important human domains like morality, religion, ethics, and animal law might be pertinent to modern practices that the veterinary profession supports (such as factory farming). The upshot is that talk about animal rights is often discouraged on veterinary school campuses.

This is troubling, since discussions of ethics are essential to effective learning about animals, whether human or nonhuman. Such discussions supply important openness and critical thinking, both of which are needed in any good education. Further, ethics-based discussions are needed in particular when the science community slips into habits of harming animals because that community is financially reliant on government, industry, and political patronage.

But science has so often been open to other animals that it can be said to be "friendly" to animal rights in one very significant sense. That sense is evident in this passage from Alexandra Horowitz's *Inside of a Dog*.

We do no disservice to dogs by stepping away from the leash and considering them scientifically. Their abilities and point of view merit special attention. And the result is magnificent: far from being distanced by science, we are brought closer to and can marvel at the true nature of the dog. Used rigorously but creatively, the process and results of science can shed new light on discussions that people have daily about what their dog knows, understands, or believes. Through my personal journey, learning to look systematically and scientifically at my own dog's behavior, I came to have a better understanding of, appreciation of, and relationship with her.

This passage makes it clear that *modern sciences open us up to the world and its nonhuman animals.* The objectivity aimed at by sciences does not erase realities like the intelligence, personality, and emotions of other animals, but it provides carefully documented recognition of their inevitable role and presence in other animals' lives. This is one reason sciences of all kinds can be—indeed, must be—in dialogue with ethics-based endeavors. It is only a combination of these two—that is, an effort that is scientifically literate, even as it is also ethically literate and sensitive—that can create an approach that is a win-win for humans and nonhumans alike.

Animal rights as a general movement benefits from healthy, open-minded science communities, even as it insists that all of us must pay attention to the ways in which ethics is, always has been, and will surely remain an integral part of human existence. Animal rights is thus an area where ethics and science must be in constant dialogue.

Arguing in this manner is not to force everyone to learn the sometimes jargonized, even sterile approaches found too often in the academic field called "ethics." That field has, as noted in chapter 3, made wonderful contributions to the modern animal rights movement. But the ethical insight that drives animal rights generally is extremely simple and straightforward. It is the practical, commonsense insight that humans have the special ability to care about others, to meet them as they are, to take them seriously as living beings. In essence, the animal rights movement constantly asks the fundamental question of all ethics, namely, "who are the others about whom I might care?"

What we do with this question—as individuals, as members of communal and charitable organizations, as shareholders of corporations, as voters in local elections, and as citizens of the world—is the subject of the next five subsections.

What is the role of the individual citizen?

The individual citizen has a central role in bringing about the future, given that our choices can, as has already been suggested, "celebrate the world we want." This is particularly true for those who live in consumer-oriented societies that contribute so much to contemporary problems like pollution, habitat destruction, and global warming. Without such individuals helping, animal protection of any form will be difficult.

Since the individual is the key component of the groups we discuss in the next four topics, we return to this level of ethical responsibility after considering the role of nonprofit groups, corporations, local government, and national and international governments.

What is the role of nonprofit organizations?

By virtue of the fact that individuals already have a certain power, people working *together* on specific issues magnify by many fold the power of individuals that leads to the hopeful observation, "Never doubt that a small group of committed citizens can change the world." Thus, while revolutions may indeed be hard to start, the processes that lead to fundamental changes can best be started by individuals as part of a group of people working together.

What is the role of corporations?

There are many calls today to create public policies that enhance corporate social responsibility. This is a welcome trend for the reasons suggested by Paul Hawken in this passage from *Blessed Unrest: How the Largest Movement in the World Came into Being, and Why No One Saw It Coming.* He is speaking about the important legal rights and freedoms businesses have been accorded in order to operate and make a profit.

> Business justifies these rights because of its indisputable argument that it creates value, a position that nevertheless neatly evades the other side of the issue: How much value does it destroy in the process of carrying out its activities? ... Rachel Carson's reluctant conclusion was that once-respected businesses were creating products that destroyed value. They were exceeding their license to operate, and creating a public health hazard that threatened the web of life. Business rights are illegitimate if they remove rights from others, if they are not reciprocal and mutual with the rights of citizens, and if they extirpate other forms of life.

Getting for-profit businesses involved in social movements is no easy matter, but since business interests can impact policy, they are necessary dialogue partners if animal protectionists and society in general are to move in the direction of effective moral and/or legal protections for living beings outside of our own species. One strategy for prompting businesses to act in animal-friendly ways is related to the fact that individual citizens ultimately own the shares of for-profit corporate entities. Another is to use consumer pressure to push businesses to act in socially responsible ways. Both strategies are important to recognizing how the public must *and can* guide corporations as they impact future possibilities in protecting other living beings of all kinds.

What is the role of municipalities and villages and other local communities?

This is presently one of the most important levels of creativity available in animal protection, environmental, and social justice matters. Not only are communal values worked out at this important government level, but decisions on land and energy use, animal control issues, and recycling possibilities are characteristically controlled locally. Perhaps most important, the specifics of education are often determined locally.

Crucial for consideration at this level are not only local problems—like shelters for companion animals or environmental practices and wildlife management—but also the local community's role in promoting discussion and resolution of national and international issues. Solutions at this "lower" level of government impact what is seen and done locally, and this creates grassroots pressure and political consensus for meaningful protections at the national and international levels.

What is the role of provinces, states, and countries in animal protection?

As the principal policy makers in modern, industrialized, and industrializing societies, *our* governments at this level shape the world in which our children will live. Further, because humans are such a force on the earth today, decisions at regional and national levels profoundly impact the rest of life on Earth. Individuals often feel powerless to control such large entities, but in the early twenty-first century the power of individuals and small groups has been greatly enhanced by cost-effective technology like the Internet. Grassroots movements thus are key, as are votes at the ballot box and in the marketplace. All of these increasingly important acts can impact policy-making decisions at the regional and national levels.

This observation returns us to the individual, for leaders of any social movement are necessarily individuals. The question with which to conclude this book about animals rights is this: *who will the leaders be?* Various sections have mentioned the leadership potential of lawyers, judges, legislators, teachers, education administrators, businesspeople, consumers, non-profit volunteers, elected representatives, members of religious traditions, scientists and many others. Each of these roles is filled by human individuals.

Collectively, *our species* is helpfully thought of, as Aldo Leopold suggested, not as "conqueror of the land-community" but, instead, "a *plain member and citizen* of it." Equally, *individuals* are also plain members and citizens of the land-community. This is the genius of grassroots organizing—it is the entire human community that makes a difference in other lives, human and nonhuman alike. When an individual or the whole human community chooses animal rights, that choice is, in a very real sense, about not only nonhuman animals, though they are its organizing focus. Such a choice is also about human animals as we attempt to find healthy ways for individuals in local places, and our species as a whole, to coexist with the citizens of the more-than-human world within which we and our children will always live.

TIME LINE/CHRONOLOGY
OF IMPORTANT EVENTS

Humans have been interacting with nonhumans in many different contexts for a very long time. Animal protection sentiments appear not only very early in our recorded history but were obviously part of our prehistory as well. The list that follows is confined to three dozen major dates—there are histories in the suggested readings that provide much more detail.

35,000–15,000 years ago Humans begin drawing pictures of other animals on rocks and cave walls (a well-known example is the Lascaux caves in France). Since the depicted animals are not always those that were hunted, the drawings suggest to some an honoring of the connection with, perhaps even identification between, humans and the depicted animals.

15,000 years ago Humans begin making the transition from a hunting-gathering lifestyle to pastoral and agricultural ways of life. Transition to domestication of animals and plants changed the relationship to animals, to land, and to each other.

12,000–10,000 B.C.E. Practice of burying or other forms of ritual disposing of dead dogs and some other animals can be found around the world.

7,000 B.C.E. Some cultures in Asia have domesticated donkeys, sheep, pigs, and goats. By 4,000–5,000 years ago the humans of southwestern Asia had domesticated virtually all of the livestock and crop plants that are central to Old World cultures.

900–200 B.C.E. Religions go through their Axial Age, in which ethical concern for both humans and nonhumans are a major factor

400–325 B.C.E. Plato in the *Timaeus* portrays women and other animals as failed men. But he does not deny completely that other animals can think, even reason in some ways.

350–300 B.C.E. Lively debate in the Greek world over other animals' abilities. Aristotle denies reason to other animals but pioneers a systematic approach to other animals in encyclopedic works that will be standard work on animals for more than 1,500 years.

300 B.C.E. to 200 C.E. The philosophers known as Stoics downgrade the behavior of other animals generally, and some Greeks, including the Greek physician Galen in Rome, perform animal experiments.

400 C.E. The Stoic dismissal of nonhuman animals is advanced by the central Christian figure Augustine of Hippo and thereby becomes embedded in Western, Latin-speaking Christianity. In this way, the anti-animal half of a very lively and more balanced ancient debate prevailed.

1200 Francis of Assisi becomes renown for his Christian appreciation of nonhuman animals.

1550s The first depiction of vivisection appears in a woodcut by Vesalius portraying Galen dissecting a pig.

1625–1700 René Descartes, who died in 1650, advances views of other animals as machines.

1641 Massachusetts Bay Colony passes law addressing issue of animal welfare.

1700s Voltaire replies to Descartes, "Answer me, you who believe that animals are only machines. Has nature arranged for this animal to have all the machinery of feelings only in order for it not to have any at all?"

1762 First veterinary school in western culture founded in Lyons, France, to help the French army avoid diseases among its horses needed for cavalry and to pull cannons.

1747 The founder of the modern science of taxonomy, Carolus Linnaeus, asks in a letter, "What is the difference between man and ape, based on natural history? Most definitely I see no difference. I wish some one could show me even one distinction."

1776 The Englishman Humphrey Primatt publishes *The Duty of Mercy and the Sin of Cruelty to Brute Animals.*

1789 Bentham publishes *An Introduction to the Principles of Morals and Legislation* and starts tradition of utilitarian philosophy looking at nonhuman issues with his famous observation, "The question is not, Can they *reason?* nor, Can they *talk?* but, Can they *suffer?*"

1792 Mary Wollstonecraft publishes her classic *A Vindication of the Rights of Women,* and in the same year Thomas Taylor responds with *A Vindication of the Rights of Beasts* as a parody of the claim that women have "intrinsic and real dignity and worth."

1822 English parliament passes "An Act to prevent the cruel and improper Treatment of Cattle," known today as Martin's Act and one of the first pieces of animal rights legislation. The act protected working and farm animals—"ox, cow, heifer, steer, sheep, or other cattle."

1840–1900 Societies for Prevention of Cruelty to Animals pioneered in England, and then appear in many other parts of the world.

1859 Charles Darwin publishes *On the Origin of Species,* which quickly generates a debate that continues to this day about both other animals' abilities and humans' relationship to other living beings.

1870s–1890s Animal experimentation is the subject of, but ultimately survives, a powerful anti-vivisection campaign in England led primarily by Christian clergy.

1892 Henry Salt publishes *Animals' Rights Considered in Relation to Social Progress.*

1913 John B. Watson publishes article "Psychology as the Behaviorist Views It," which is often referred to as "The Behaviorist Manifesto" because it attempts "a purely objective experimental branch of natural science." Although Watson suggested that behaviorism "recognizes no dividing line between man and brute," the philosophy became the established position in science until late in the twentieth century because it could be used to deny mind, emotions, and any mental complexity in nonhuman animals.

1930 Darwinian synthesis A new era in Darwin-influenced thinking begins in which mathematical ideas are combined with genetics-based ideas of inheritance. Also called neo-Darwinism, this set of ideas about humans' relationship to other living beings has become the prevailing view of scientists today.

1948 The Constitution of India goes into effect—in its "Fundamental Duties" section it provides, "It shall be the duty of every citizen of India ... to have compassion for living creatures."

1966 The pioneering Animal Welfare Act is enacted in the United States. Amended significantly in 1985 to create procedures for review of experiments, this law covers many animals, but government regulators on their own exclude rats and mice. Many other countries adopt such laws and cover even rats and mice.

1970 The first Earth Day (April 22) reveals the appeal of the environmental movement.

1975 Publication of Peter Singer's *Animal Liberation*

1977 The first course in animal law is taught at Seton Hall Law School in the United States.

1980s–1990s Genetic engineering begins to take off.

1993 The Great Ape Project calls for "equality beyond humanity."

1997–1998 Fundamental laws of the European Union (the Treaty of Amsterdam and the Treaty of Rome) refer to nonhuman animals as "sentient beings."

2000 Harvard Law School adopts an animal law course because of student demand, and within a decade student petitions at a majority of American law schools have resulted in similar courses. Many law schools in other countries are adopted at this time as well.

2002 German constitution amended in order to elevate protection of nonhuman animals to the most fundamental level.

GLOSSARY

Words make a difference, for as many people know and as philosophers have long observed, they can bewitch us. But words can also liberate us *if* we use them carefully. This glossary includes definitions from a variety of sources because so many people today want to not only participate but even to control the animal rights debate. So the entries below, whose source is identified if they come from someone other than the author, range from simple, common-sense definitions to agenda-driven definitions. The latter come from liberation groups, government farm bureaus, veterinary associations, and even the Web site of a radical wing of today's incredibly varied animal protection movement.

abolition   "Total elimination, versus the reform, of some form of oppression, enslavement, or abuse." (from the Web site of the Animal Liberation Front)

animal   Two definitions are typically featured in dictionaries. The first and more general is usually the scientific definition, which includes humans as animals. The second is the more common but nonscientific use of "animals" to mean all other living beings, as in the phrase "humans and animals."

animal law   A field of legal education and scholarship around the world that first emerged in the 1970s.

animal rights   Defined in a wide variety of ways, this term originally referred to the long-standing tradition that originated in religious traditions suggesting that each human should act in ways that, to the extent he or she can, take into consideration the interests of the living beings outside human species. In recent years, the term has also come to mean use of legal protections for other living beings.

(1) "A philosophy that animals have the same rights as people. They want to end the use of animals as companions and pets. In extreme cases, they oppose the use of animals for food, fiber, entertainment, and medical research." (from Web site of Pennsylvania Farm Bureau)

(2) "Animal rights, also referred to as animal liberation, is the idea that the most basic interests of animals should be afforded the same consideration as the similar interests of humans." (*Encyclopaedia Britannica*)

animal welfare Another term that is defined in many different ways. There is a weak sense of the term that refers to any improvement whatsoever in the condition of animals being harmed by humans. There is a far more substantial idea of animal welfare centering on animals being free from harms like captivity and pain, as well as being afforded the freedom to move around.

(1) "Animal welfare is the ethical responsibility of ensuring animal well-being. Animal well-being is the condition in which animals experience good health, are able to effectively cope with their environment, and are able to express a diversity of species-typical behaviors. Protecting an animal's welfare means providing for its physical and mental needs." (from the Web site of the American Veterinary Medical Association)

(2) "Animal welfare is the physical and psychological state of non-human animals." (C. Hewson in *The Canadian Veterinary Journal*)

cruelty free A term common in discussions about consumer products that refers to production of those products or the existence of certain animal-related practices that attempt to eliminate intentional cruelty and harm to the animals involved.

companion animal A synonym for "pet," the term is usually a reference to those animals kept for companionship and enjoyment or as a member of a household.

"A replacement for the word "pet" in the animal-rights lexicon, designed to be more palatable to legislators and judges looking for easy ways to grant animals additional rights. Where "pet" is considered patronizing, "companion" suggests a relationship of equality." (from the anti-animal rights Web site animalscam .com)

euthanasia   The original meaning was "an easy or happy death," derived from the Greek words *eu* ("good") and *thanatos* ("death"). The first use of the term to mean "legally sanctioned mercy killing" (which happened even when the animal was healthy) was in 1869.

factory farming   Synonyms are "industrialized agriculture," "intensive agriculture," and CAFO (a U.S. government term that means "confined animal feeding operations")—this is a reference to the general style of production found in production facilities for food animals, which became common in the 1980s.

intrinsic value   A term used by both philosophers and marketing people, this is a reference to the commonsense idea that something (it could be a living being or an object) has value "in itself" as an intrinsic property and not because of its values to others, such as humans.

legal rights   Specific, fundamental legal protections always originating within a specific legal system and characteristically spelled out in a statute, regulation, or court decision.

moral rights   Protections anchored in any of the many moral systems that humans have used—a much vaguer term than "legal right."

sentience   The capacity of some living beings for sensations, such as pain. The term sometimes is used as a synonym for "conscious" or "aware," but most uses of the term refer to the basic fact that a living being is capable of experiencing, sensing, feeling.

speciesism   Coined in 1970 by Richard Ryder (a prominent member of Britain's Royal Society for the Prevention of Cruelty to Animals), the term refers to use of membership in the human species as the sole criterion for deciding which living beings deserve fundamental protections—the positive side of the term is that any and all members of human species are recognized as important, while the negative side of the term is exclusion of any and all nonhuman animals from such protections.

utilitarianism   "The doctrine which states that the rightness and wrongness of actions is determined by the goodness and badness of their consequences." (*The Encyclopedia of Philosophy*)

vegan   "Ways of living that seek to exclude, as far as is possible and practical, all forms of exploitation of animals for food, clothing or any other purpose." (British Vegan Society)

vivisection   An older term that originally meant the act of operating on living animals (especially in scientific research), this term, which comes from the Latin words *vivus* ("alive") and *sectio* ("cutting"), sometimes now is used by animal protectionists to cover any invasive experiment involving nonhuman animals. The term "vivisector" is almost always meant as a scathing criticism.

SUGGESTIONS FOR FURTHER READING

1. General Information

Magel, Charles R., ed., 1989. *A Keyguide to Information Sources in Animal Rights*. London: Mansell Publishing.

Singer, Peter, ed., 1985. *In Defence of Animals*. New York: Basil Blackwell.

2. The Animals Themselves

Bekoff, Marc, and John A. Byers. 1998. *Animal Play: Evolutionary, Comparative, and Ecological Perspectives*. Cambridge [England]: Cambridge University Press.

Bekoff, Marc. 2007. *The Emotional Lives of Animals: A Leading Scientist Explores Animal Joy, Sorrow, and Empathy—and Why They Matter*. Novato, Calif.: New World Library.

Bekoff, Marc, and Jessica Pierce. 2009. *Wild Justice: The Moral Lives of Animals*. Chicago: University of Chicago Press.

Bekoff, Marc. 2010. *Encyclopedia of Animal Rights and Animal Welfare*. Santa Barbara, Calif.: Greenwood Press.

Griffin, Donald R. 1981. *The Question of Animal Awareness: Evolutionary Continuity of Mental Experience*. New York: Rockefeller University Press.

Griffin, Donald R. 2001. *Animal Minds: Beyond Cognition to Consciousness*, Chicago: University of Chicago Press. Revised edition of *Animal Minds*, 1992.

Horowitz, Alexandra. 2009. *Inside of a Dog: What Dogs See, Smell, and Know*. New York: Scribner.

Lorenz, Konrad Z. 1952. *King Solomon's Ring*, trans. by Marjorie Latzke. New York: Thomas Y. Crowell.

Lorenz, Konrad Z. 1966. *On Aggression*, trans. by Marjorie Kerr Wilson. London: Methuen.

Tinbergen, Niko. 1972. *The Animal in Its World: Explorations of an Ethologist, 1932–1972*. Cambridge, Mass.: Harvard University Press.

Wilson, E. O. 1984. *Biophilia*. Cambridge, Mass., and London: Harvard University Press.

Wilson, E. O. 1992. *The Diversity of Life*. Cambridge, Mass.: The Belknap Press of Harvard University Press.

Wise. Steven M. 2002. *Drawing the Line: Science and the Case for Animal Rights*. Cambridge, Mass.: Perseus.

3. Philosophical Arguments

DeGrazia, David. 1996. *Taking Animals Seriously: Mental Life and Moral Status*. Cambridge and New York, Cambridge University Press.

Nussbaum, Martha Craven. 2006. *Frontiers of Justice: Disability, Nationality, Species Membership*. Cambridge, Mass.: Harvard University Press.

Regan, Tom. 1983. *The Case for Animal Rights*. Berkeley: University of California Press.

Rollin, Bernard E. 1981. *Animal Rights and Human Morality*. Buffalo, N.Y.: Prometheus Books.

Rollin, Bernard E. 1998. *The Unheeded Cry: Animal Consciousness, Animal Pain, and Science*. Ames: Iowa State University Press.

Schweitzer, Albert. 1923. *Civilization and Ethics. The Philosophy of Civilization*. The Dale Memorial Lectures, 1922.

Singer, Peter. 1998. *Ethics into Action: Henry Spira and the Animal Rights Movement*. New York: Rowman & Littlefield.

Singer, Peter. 1975. *Animal Liberation: A New Ethics for Our Treatment of Animals*. New York: New York Review Book/Random House. The 2nd edition came out in 1990 (New York: Avon Books).

4. History and Culture

Adams, Carol. 1991. *The Sexual Politics of Meat: A Feminist-Vegetarian Critical Theory*. New York: Continuum.

Adams, Carol J., and Josephine Donovan. 1995. *Animals and Women: Feminist Theoretical Explorations*. Durham, N.C.: Duke University Press.

Anderson, Virginia DeJohn. 2004. *Creatures of Empire: How Domestic Animals Transformed Early America*. New York: Oxford University Press.

Beers, Diane L. 2006. *For the Prevention of Cruelty: The History and Legacy of Animal Rights Activism in the United States*. Athens: Swallow Press/Ohio University Press.

Chapple, Christopher Key. 1993. *Nonviolence to Animals, Earth, and Self in Asian Traditions*. Albany: State University of New York Press.

Darnton, Robert. 2000. *The Great Cat Massacre: And Other Episodes in French Cultural History*. New York: BasicBooks.

Foltz, Richard. 2006. *Animals in Islamic Tradition and Muslim Cultures*. Oxford [England]: Oneworld.

Gold, Mark. 1995. *Animal Rights: Extending the Circle of Compassion*. Oxford [England]: Jon Carpenter.

Hobgood-Oster, Laura. 2008. *Holy Dogs and Asses: Animals in the Christian Tradition*. Urbana: University of Illinois Press.

Kalof, Linda, and Brigitte Pohl-Resl. 2007. *A Cultural History of Animals*. Oxford, UK: Berg.

Kean, Hilda. 1998. *Animal Rights: Political and Social Change in Britain Since 1800*. London: Reaktion Books.

Linzey, Andrew, and Tom Regan. 1988. *Animals and Christianity: A Book of Readings*. New York: Crossroad.

Preece, Rod. 1999. *Animals and Nature: Cultural Myths, Cultural Realities*. Vancouver: UBC Press.

Preece, Rod. 2005. *Brute Souls, Happy Beasts, and Evolution: The Historical Status of Animals*. Vancouver: UBC Press.

Sax, Boria. 2000. *Animals in the Third Reich: Pets, Scapegoats, and the Holocaust*. New York: Continuum.

Shevelow, Kathryn. 2008. *For the Love of Animals: The Rise of the Animal Protection Movement*. New York: Henry Holt and Co.

Sorabji, Richard. 1993. *Animal Minds and Human Morals: The Origins of the Western Debate*. Ithaca, N.Y.: Cornell University Press.

Thomas, Keith. 1984. *Man and the Natural World: Changing Attitudes in England 1500–1800*. New York: Pantheon.

Waldau, Paul. 2002. *The Specter of Speciesism: Buddhist and Christian Views of Animals*. American Academy of Religion Academy Series. New York: Oxford University Press.

Waldau, Paul, and Kimberley C. Patton. 2009. *A Communion of Subjects: Animals in Religion, Science, and Ethics*. New York: Columbia University Press.

Most of the books, articles and Web sites listed here advance the position that animal protection has been and now is an integral part of human life. Two books which challenge modern forms of animal rights as a dilution of this ancient movement are (1) *Animal Rights: The Inhumane Crusade* by Daniel T. Oliver (1999) and *The Hijacking of the Humane Movement: Animal Extremism* by Rod and Patti Strand (1993). A book challenging the animal welfare movement as a betrayal of the animal rights movement is the 1996 volume *Rain Without Thunder: The Ideology of the Animal Rights Movement* by Gary L. Francione.

5. Laws (Web sites where laws can be searched are listed after articles and books)

Curnutt, Jordan. 2001. *Animals and the Law*, Santa Barbara, Calif.: ABC-CLIO.

Food and Agriculture Organization (FAO), United Nations. 2002. "Legal Trends in Wildlife Management" by M.T. Cirelli in the FAO series "FAO Legislative Studies" (available for download at http://www.fao.org/docrep/005/y3844e/y3844e04.htm).

Freyfogle, E. T., and D. Goble. 2009. *Wildlife Law: A Primer*. Washington, D.C.: Island Press.

India, Maneka Gandhi, Ozair Husain, and Raj Panjwani. 2006. *Animal Laws of India*. Delhi: Universal Law.

Sunstein, Cass R., and Martha Craven Nussbaum. 2004. *Animal Rights: Current Debates and New Directions*. New York: Oxford University Press.

Wagman, Bruce A., Sonia Waisman, and Pamela D. Frasch. 2010. *Animal Law: Cases and Materials*. Durham, N.C.: Carolina Academic Press.

Wise, Steven M. 2000. *Rattling the Cage: Toward Legal Rights for Animals*, Cambridge, Mass.: Merloyd Lawrence/Perseus.

Web Sites

Animal Legal & Historical Web Center—www.animallaw.info

Animal Legal Defense Fund—www.aldf.org

Ancient law information is available at http://www.animalrightshistory .org/index.htm

Center for Animal Law Studies—www.lclark.edu/law/centers/animal_ law_studies/

International—Animal protection laws in various countries can be researched at www.uni-giessen.de/tierschutz/and general law materials for other countries are at the Web site of the Global Legal Information Network(GLIN), lcweb2.1oc.gov/law/GLINv1/GLIN .html.

International Institute for Animal Law—www.animallawintl.org/index .htm

6. Political Realities and 7. Social Realities

Fearn, Eva, Kent, Hubbard Redford, and Ward Woods. 2010. *State of the Wild: A Global Portrait*. Washington, D.C.: Island Press.

Garner, Robert. 1998. *Political Animals: Animal Protection Politics in Britain and the United States*. New York: St. Martin's.

Salem, Deborah J., and Andrew N. Rowan. 2001. *The State of the Animals*. 2001. Washington, D.C.: Humane Society Press.

Salem, Deborah J., and Andrew N. Rowan. 2001. *The State of the Animals II*. 2003. Washington, D.C.: Humane Society Press.

Salem, Deborah J., and Andrew N. Rowan. 2005. *The State of the Animals III*. 2005. Washington, D.C.: Humane Society Press.

Salem, Deborah J., and Andrew N. Rowan. 2007. *The State of the Animals IV*, 2007. Washington, D.C.: Humane Society Press.

Schlosser, Eric. 2001. *Fast Food Nation: The Dark Side of the All-American Meal*. Boston: Houghton Mifflin.

Scully, Matthew. 2003. *Dominion: The Power of Man, the Suffering of Animals, and the Call to Mercy*. New York: St. Martin's.

State of the Wild: A Global Portrait of Wildlife, Wildlands, and Oceans. 2008. Washington, D.C.: Island Press.

8. Education, the Professions, and the Arts

Aftandilian, David. 2007. *What Are the Animals to Us?: Approaches from Science, Religion, Folklore, Literature, and Art*. Knoxville: University of Tennessee Press.

Bekoff, Marc. 2000. *Strolling with Our Kin: Speaking for and Respecting Voiceless Animals*. New York: Lantern Books.

Bekoff, Marc 2002. *Minding Animals: Toward Heartfelt Encounters with Our Animal Kin*. New York: Oxford University Press.

Louv, Richard. 2005. *Last Child in the Woods: Saving Our Children from Nature-Deficit Disorder*. Chapel Hill, N.C.: Algonquin Books of Chapel Hill.

Sax, Boria. 2001. *The Mythical Zoo: An A–Z of Animals in World Myth, Legend, and Literature*, Santa Barbara, Calif.: ABC-CLIO.

Weil, Zoe. 2003. *Above All, Be Kind: Raising a Humane Child in Challenging Times*. Gabriola Island, B.C.: New Society Publishers.

Weil, Zoe. 2004. *The Power and Promise of Humane Education*. Gabriola Island, B.C.: New Society Publishers.

9. Contemporary Sciences—Natural and Social (see chapter 2 references as well)

Allen, Collin, and Marc Bekoff, 1997. *Species of Mind: The Philosophy and Biology of Cognitive Ethology*, Cambridge, Mass.: Bradford/MIT Press.

Rollin, Bernard E. 2006. *Science and Ethics*. Cambridge, Mass.: Cambridge University Press.

10. Major Figures and Organizations in the Animal Rights Movement

Kok, Wim de. 1999. *World Animal Net Directory: International Directory of Animal Protection Organisations*. Boston: World Animal Net, Inc.

INDEX